What No One Ever Tells You About

MARKETING YOUR OWN BUSINESS

Jan Norman

Dearborn™
Trade Publishing
A **Kaplan Professional** Company

This publication is designed to provide accurate and authoritative information in regard to the subject matter covered. It is sold with the understanding that the publisher is not engaged in rendering legal, accounting, or other professional service. If legal advice or other expert assistance is required, the services of a competent professional should be sought.

Vice President and Publisher: Cynthia A. Zigmund
Acquisitions Editor: Michael Cunningham
Senior Project Editor: Trey Thoelcke
Interior Design: Lucy Jenkins
Cover Design: Scott Rattray, Rattray Design
Typesetting: Elizabeth Pitts

Published by Dearborn Trade Publishing
A Kaplan Professional Company

04 05 06 10 9 8 7 6 5 4 3 2 1

Library of Congress Cataloging-in-Publication Data

Norman, Jan.
  What no one ever tells you about marketing your own business : real-life advice from 101 successful entrepreneurs / Jan Norman.
    p.   cm.
  Includes index.
  ISBN 0-7931-8572-6
  1. Marketing. I. Title.
  HF5415.N67   2004
  658.8—dc22

                                                          2004003270

Dearborn Trade books are available at special quantity discounts to use for sales promotions, employee premiums, or educational purposes. Please call our Special Sales Department to order or for more information at 800-245-2665, e-mail trade@dearborn.com, or write to Dearborn Trade Publishing, 30 South Wacker Drive, Suite 2500, Chicago, IL 60606-7481.

DEDICATION

To my father, Howard Norman, the first entrepreneur I ever knew

CONTENTS

If you want to go out of business, stop marketing.

Of course, that's not your aim. You want to build a strong and lasting business for personal and societal good. Marketing is essential to achieve that goal. It's unfortunate that some people think marketing is bad. That attitude probably stems from misunderstanding what marketing is or thinking of marketing as just a small slice of the activities it actually encompasses. A few companies that misuse and abuse their marketing add to the misperception. Marketing is everything a company is and does. A company's ethics, culture, work environment, hiring practices, attention to quality, and customer service all affect and are affected by marketing. The more you appreciate the interconnectedness of various elements of your business, the better your marketing will become.

It is noteworthy how often the people interviewed for this book stressed the need for honesty and ethical behavior in order for marketing—and their companies—to be successful. Some companies spend a lot of money on and attention to logos and clever advertising, ignoring the damage done by unethical behavior. The lesson? Build your business and marketing on a foundation of integrity. This book is not about the theory of marketing. It's about how real businesses have used some of the primary marketing techniques and tools in real life. Although 101 examples are detailed in these pages, thousands more have been used successfully through the ages, and creative business marketers are dreaming up more all the time. Your marketing will be limited only by your imagination and resources.

Perhaps the marketing factor mentioned most often by the business marketers in these pages is the importance of relationships. Most striking is how many different ways relationships intersect with marketing. As you will read more than once in this book, people do business with people they know, like, and trust. Your ability to strengthen human relationships through marketing will determine the success of your business. However, befriending every person within ten miles of your business isn't the solution. The most common mistake novice business owners make is trying to be all things to all people. They think everyone can use their product or service. Perhaps they're right. But even Bill Gates doesn't have enough time and money to market to everyone who can use his software. If he did, even Microsoft wouldn't be able to satisfy everyone. In fact, it doesn't. You need to identify your most likely customers: the people who already know they need your product or service so that you don't have to spend marketing dollars to educate them, who have the money, and who are ready to make a decision. It's a bonus if these people also know why they should buy from you instead of all the other options out there. But that's what marketing should explain. The tendency to try to please everyone usually reflects insecurity more than greed. You're afraid that turning customers away will hurt your business. Relax. Businesses succeed daily filling the need or solving the problem of a sliver of the marketplace.

The most useful tool in alleviating that anxiety is the marketing plan. Just as the business plan is the road map for the direction of the overall company, the marketing plan coordinates all the marketing elements. By thinking through these issues in advance, you become more comfortable rejecting the nice people and interesting opportunities that are outside the plan at the moment. Your company should have a marketing plan. Each product or service should have a separate marketing plan. Each marketing campaign should have its own plan as well.

Many business owners became enthralled with and then disenchanted by the Internet in marketing. You need to balance your enthusiasm and skepticism. The Internet's influence is growing and must not be ignored. But it is a tool just like every other element of marketing. The Internet can improve customer service and build relationships, but it does none of these things by itself. Stick to your marketing plan, which will craft a balanced and comprehensive approach to reaching the right customers with the right message at the right time.

An important factor to understand about marketing is that nothing works all the time for all products and services in all circumstances and in every economy. That's why it is important to continually monitor your marketing, track its results, and make adjustments for greatest efficiency and effectiveness. Perhaps you will apply one or more of the ideas from this book in your marketing. If an idea doesn't work, analyze why. Adjust it or drop it. Equally important is understanding that no one tactic, strategy, or campaign will bring marketing success by itself. Every one of the companies in these pages uses many different marketing tools and techniques. Just one is highlighted for each chapter to help readers better understand how each element has worked in the real world. But realize that each tool is part of a larger, coordinated marketing effort.

Because marketing is fundamental to your business success, it is wise to adopt the attitude that you're going to enjoy it. Many successful entrepreneurs have acknowledged that they entered business dreading the idea of marketing, but once they determined to do it the best they could, they enjoyed marketing and the customers and friends they made. The enjoyment is one of the most significant rewards of running your own business.

ACKNOWLEDGMENTS

I am deeply indebted to all the people who shared the details of their marketing successes in hopes that they may help others who are pursuing the American Dream of business success. I especially appreciate the help of my brother, Jim Norman, executive director of the Phoenix Creative Planning Centers Foundation, Inc., who so generously connected me with his network of entrepreneurs. This is grassroots marketing at its best.

I also thank Suzanne Martin, Barry Schnitt, Steven Toole, Christine Ragasa, and the U.S. Small Business Administration for helping me find small business owners with wonderful stories to share.

PART 1

BEFORE YOU START MARKETING

■ ■ ■

You're all pumped up. You're ready to print and distribute some fliers or take out an ad. But wait. The difference between stab-in-the-dark marketing and the most effective and efficient marketing is the foundation you lay beneath your entire business. Marketing has some aspects that novices don't realize. How you market your business depends on the kind of company you create.

The impatient marketer may read these chapters and wonder, "That's marketing?" Yes, everything about your business is marketing.

The ethics and culture you cultivate within your business form the most important foundation upon which all other aspects of marketing will build. Get this part right and you're well on your way to success. Get it wrong and no amount of marketing will correct or cover over the faults. Similarly, the level of quality to which you commit will define your company and the market you will pursue. No business, not even Wal-mart or Microsoft, can be all things to all people, so the niche you choose and the customers you identify as your target will greatly shape your marketing. To effectively satisfy them, you must understand how they think, what they need, and what motivates them. You also need to study your competitors, especially their weaknesses and oversights that give you a wedge into the market, which circles back to the niche you choose. See how these various aspects of your business are related? These foundational elements should come together in the strategy that keeps everyone within your company on the same page and drives the business forward to success.

1. THE VERY FOUNDATION OF MARKETING

To succeed for the long term, a company must
build its marketing on ethics and honesty.

■ ■ ■

Pete Maddox builds, repairs, and maintains computer systems for companies. He keeps their building and office keys so that he can work at nights and weekends in order to be the least disruptive to their work. He solves costly computer problems that will save his clients money over time, even though it eliminates work that would bring him substantial income.

Ethics and honesty are the basis of Pete's company—Commerce Technologies LLC in Santa Ana, California—and his marketing. Some business owners don't think ethics and marketing are related. But an elaborate marketing plan or clever marketing tactic that is not ethical or honest cannot successfully promote a company for long. Ethics form the foundation for all marketing and permeate every action, relationship, and campaign. If you apply to your business only one lesson from this book, make it this one: Companies built to last have a strong ethical foundation and honest marketing practices.

Pete's foundation and practice are simple: "I work in the best interest of my clients, period."

He doesn't leave a job until it's finished, and sometimes he works all weekend to resolve a problem. He won't recommend changing technology products unless it improves employee productivity and is absolutely reliable. If a computer-dependent client suffers a catastrophic system failure, Pete loans the client a complete system and servers free of charge while he restores the regular system.

"I understand that if their network is down, they're out of business," he says. "If a client pages me with a 911, I leave a meeting or an appointment and immediately handle the problem. Of course, all of my clients know that I'll do the same for them, so they're not upset when I say I have to leave because a system is down."

Occasionally, he develops money-saving solutions that reduce his billable hours. Among Pete's clients are a tropical plant distributor and a sheet-metal fabricator whose environments are so dirty that they were spending $800 a month for Pete to clean their computers. "I viewed this as a good profit center for me, but an unnecessarily high expense for my clients," Pete says. So he developed a low-cost computer enclosure with reusable automotive filters. Clients could eliminate their cleaning costs and reduce other service calls to repair hardware problems with floppy drives, CD-ROMs, and tape backups that are especially vulnerable to dirt.

Is that marketing? Consider this, Pete has virtually no client turnover and no problems with clients reluctant to pay. Pete considers every client relationship a partnership. One long-time, technology-related client lost much of its business in the dot-com bust. Pete reduced his monthly retainer although he continued to work the same hours. "We grow together and suffer together," he explains.

However, ethical behavior is a two-way street, and Pete has learned to end business relationships if the client is dishonest or abusive. The ethical businessperson isn't a doormat. "America is founded on ideals, and things go wrong when you ignore those ideals, even the little ones," Pete says. "When you work in clients' best interest, everything flows from that. It isn't a separate marketing strategy; it's inherent in your whole business."

■ ■ ■

Ethics is the moral code of right and wrong incorporated into your life, whether business or personal. Before making an ethical decision:

- List the facts of the situation as clearly as possible.

- Determine who will be affected by your decision and your obligations to all concerned.

- Ask whether everyone, including you, is being treated fairly and justly. You shouldn't be the loser any more than you should be the unfair winner.

- List the potential choices that are clear to you.

- Determine how best to implement the most balanced ethical choice within your power.

- Be prepared to walk away from an unethical business situation even if it costs you.

2. CAREFULLY DEFINE YOUR BUSINESS

No business can be all things to all people. Understand your
niche before identifying your customers and how to reach them.

■ ■ ■

When it started in 1989, the clearest fact about Martin Integrated Systems in Orange, California, was that it installed ceilings. Partners Marshall "Marty" Hovivian and Ann Reizer carefully fenced within their business plan the description of the company and its mission to be the best, not necessarily the biggest. They didn't try to be general contractors. They turned down client requests to take on unrelated projects. They focused on being the best ceiling installation company. They further defined their niche as the Southern California market. Marty has accepted a few contracts in Northern California and one in Houston, Texas, but only at the request of good clients. They defined their niche even further. While every new and remodeled building needs ceilings, Martin Integrated won't install every one.

The benefit is that Martin Integrated doesn't have to spread marketing time and dollars across many different construction markets or many geographic markets.

"It's hard because you see other opportunities," Marty says. "But long-term success is like sticking your hand in a cookie jar. It's not how many cookies you can grab at one time, but how many you can handle and still get your fist out of the jar."

A clearly defined niche allows a business owner to describe the ideal customer and the most effective means for marketing to that customer. Too many fledgling entrepreneurs are afraid they won't get enough business, so they use a shotgun. Marty prefers a marksman's rifle. "I analyzed whom I wanted to do business with, and I focused on those people," he says.

Businesses are built on relationships and loyalty. That takes time and effort. If you try to corral too many close collaborations, they'll tend to be shallow and fickle. A few well-cultivated relationships provide a stronger foundation on which a company can stand in good times and bad. Marty concentrated his efforts on the premier general contractors.

"I also focused on being a specialty ceiling company," Marty says. "We're only as good as our last job." The company has installed ceilings in high-rise office towers, the Aquarium of the Pacific, Dodger Stadium's restaurant, and headquarters for major corporations. Sticking to those customer and business niches enabled Martin Integrated to grow even during the recession of the early '90s.

"What happens to many companies is that they get bored with what they're doing and go off into something they don't know much about," Marty says. "They strip assets from the core business and as a result everything declines. You have to resist that."

A niche doesn't have to be confining if you think outside the box, he adds. A few years ago he recognized that the hospital market was a huge opportunity for him because of new legal requirements that hospitals build or retrofit to meet stricter standards. He consciously cultivated his relationships among contractors who specialize in medical and pharmaceutical construction and started winning the subcontracts for ceiling installation.

■ ■ ■

How to narrow your market for easier marketing and bigger profits:

- Carefully define your product or service. Be specific.

- Describe your ideal customer, the person or company that will make going to work a joy.

- Decide whether to fence your market geographically. Key factors include travel time and shipping costs.

- Continually refine your niche to make best use of company resources and strengths.

3. DO-IT-YOURSELF FOCUS GROUPS

A small group of potential customers can provide useful
impressions and attitudes that will improve a new
business concept and strategies for marketing it.

■ ■ ■

What do people *feel* about a new product or service you're about to take to market? Why should you care?

"People make buying decisions based on emotion," says Roderick "Rick" Bayless, partner of New Millennium Consulting in Newport Beach, California. "If buying was only a rational decision, then marketing would be only about price and features."

To get at those emotions that drive buying decisions, major consumer companies, like General Mills, use focus groups. Rick knows because has worked for General Mills among others and has personally presided over more than a hundred focus groups for dozens of industries. Focus groups provide qualitative information that helps the company focus other market research, such as large-scale surveys to get statistically valid data. "The information can help you focus so you save money, but don't make marketing decisions only on what focus groups say," Rick warns.

You don't have to have the marketing budget of General Mills to use focus groups when you're developing the concept for a new product or service and the strategies for marketing it. Even start-up ventures with a shoestring marketing budget can adopt focus-group techniques informally. One of Rick's low-cost focus groups involved a microbrewery that was in the formation stage. When a major corporation uses a focus group, it solicits six to eight targeted, likely consumers, and pays them to spend 60 to 90 minutes in a room with a one-way mirror. The company's marketing officials watch the proceedings on the blind side of the mirror. Large consumer companies have trained focus-group moderators on staff. For the microbrewery, Rick rented a modest hotel suite and called together some of his friends who had no connection to the company owners. Participants were all men who liked high-end microbrewed beers. "You don't want concept rejectors because who cares what they think," Rick says. "They're not going to buy no matter what your marketing is."

The business owner should get a moderator who is good at asking questions that draw out participants' hot buttons and feelings. "Entrepreneurs should never moderate their own focus groups," Rick says. "Entrepreneurs are passionate. They're product champions. They will try to overcome objections. But the people in the focus group don't want to argue."

Rick is a good focus group moderator because he's gregarious and has experience eliciting information from people in both the Army Rangers and CIA. Rick allowed the microbrewery founders to sit in the back of the room to listen and observe. But they were strictly warned to say nothing. Rick thinks it's important for business owners to see the proceedings so they can observe consumers' body language and hear the "wows" and "ughs." Rick started the men chatting about their general experience with and feelings about microbrewed beers in general. What did they like and not like about those beers? Why do they buy what they do? Where do they find them? If done right, focus-group members feel like they're just having a casual conversation, while the moderator is gently directing their comments toward information the company needs. After warming the group up to the general category, Rick introduced the fledgling microbrewery's concept. He asked them to sample the product and comment on sample advertisements and proposed labels.

"Don't discuss price in a focus group," he says. "Focus groups are OK for critiquing existing ideas, but don't ask them to come up with new ideas."

Professionals pay focus-group members, such as $40 for a housewife or $350 for a hard-to-get doctor. At the end of the microbrewery session, Rick gave each participant a $20 gift certificate to Border's bookstores. Such an informal session might cost several hundred dollars rather than the thousands of dollars that major corporations lay out. The shoestring effort may lack perspective and analysis that enhance the value of the raw results. But at least the entrepreneur has some information that can be tested with further market research, Rick says.

"Focus groups are part of your marketing process, not an end in themselves."

■ ■ ■

Rick's tips for focus-group preparation:

■ Identify the major objective of the session.

■ Develop five or six core questions that address features and benefits, and the potential for actually buying the product.

■ Reserve a comfortable meeting location, such as an executive suite conference room.

■ Invite potential members who are most-likely buyers

■ Three days before the session, call to remind each participant of the time, date, and place.

■ Provide nametags and refreshments.

---

4. RESEARCH THE MARKET

Understand your customers' motivation before determining the best ways to market to them.

■ ■ ■

Scott Cook, founder of Intuit Inc., didn't create Quicken financial software and then try to sell it to the public. First, he spent months talking to people who paid the family bills. Scott had watched his wife agonize over paying the bills and balancing the family checkbook, and wondered if others suffered through the monthly ritual too. He learned enough to realize he had identified a problem that he should pursue further. At the time, only 100,000 people balanced their checkbooks on personal computers. Yet personal finance is just data manipulation, at which computers excel. So Scott started telephoning residences and asking to speak to the family bill payer. He followed that process with one-on-one consumer interviews.

"I asked what they did and didn't do and why, what they liked about the process and didn't," says Scott, who cut his marketing teeth at Proctor & Gamble, consumer products giant, and at Bain & Associates, a corporate strategy firm. "You have to probe deeply. Don't accept the first answer." He followed the strategy of automaker Toyota, which had a rule of asking consumers *why* five times in order to drill down and get at consumers' root motivation, hopes, fears, and pain points. If people told Scott that they did something one way, he asked why they didn't try this other method. If they said they hated a specific task, he asked why. Scott wanted to uncover bill payers' pain. "If we just add pleasure, we don't know if people will pay. They will pay for a pain reliever," he explains.

Until a company understands its customers' motivations, it's groping in the dark to find the most effective marketing strategies and techniques. Technically oriented entrepreneurs especially tend to focus their marketing on what they have to sell rather than on what consumers want or need to buy. Armed with the results of hundreds of interviews, Scott was convinced many consumers had the same attitude toward bill paying that his wife did. He also thought computers could be a solution. So he hired college student Tom Proulx to write software that would solve bill payers' pain.

"Consumer research helps you define the problem well. And then you have to have technology that will solve it," he says.

Once Quicken was on the market, Scott created a usability lab, patterned after consumer product tactics. Consumers were asked to perform various tasks using Quicken so the company could understand how average people used its product. But even that wasn't enough. "In the lab you miss things. People only do what you tell them," Scott says. In 1990, Scott started Intuit's "Follow Me Home" program. They went into customers' homes and offices to watch not only how they used Quicken, but how they worked. The company used knowledge gained from all these methods to improve its products.

Today 22 million individuals and businesses use versions of Quicken, QuickBooks, and Turbo Tax. Intuit is, by far, the largest provider of financial software in the world, and the company continues to probe its customers' pain. Each of the 5,000 Intuit employees must talk directly with customers at least once a year. They talk with 50,000 customers annually. Intuit trains its workers to get the most out of these conversations.

"If you're going to learn something new, you have to leave your existing beliefs behind when you talk to consumers," Scott says. "The key to business success is knowing your customer."

■ ■ ■

Methods for understanding your customer:

- Talk directly with consumers by telephone, written surveys, etc.

- Study competitors' products.

- Identify psychographics of people who buy similar products.

- Watch the customer use a product.

- Continually ask, "Why?"

5.

LOOK FOR
COMPETITORS' HOLES

Before you can find a need and fill it, you must
study your competition to spot ways in which
they are not meeting market needs.

■ ■ ■

Perhaps the oldest entrepreneurial adage is find a need and fill it. This concept is described as knowing your unique selling proposition or competitive advantage. But many business owners fail to study their competitors and verbalize exactly how they stand apart from the crowd. Even many willing entrepreneurs don't know how to study their competitors.

Long-time marketing expert Michael Westlund, whose company is "Michael C. Westlund wordsmith" in Garden Grove, California, likes to use a "competition wall" to compile and analyze competitive intelligence. One client developed a highly sophisticated, computerized process control system and software for managing vast manufacturing and utility plants. Although expensive and highly flexible, the system had several competitors. Michael rounded up every piece of marketing collateral from these competitors. He also hired a clipping service to collect every advertisement, news release, and article about competitors and their products over a three-month period to make sure they missed nothing current. Michael culled the material for duplicates and posted every item on the competition wall. Then he brought together the marketing team to study the wall.

"We looked at all the messages the competitors were putting out and tried to find areas where competitors were not addressing the features and benefits our product offered," Michael says. They found two. The client's product was adaptable, while competitors forced an end user to adjust its system to the competitor's product. Second, competitors didn't address the risk involved in adopting rigid systems. "What seemed to stick out like the proverbial sore thumb was this risk factor," Michael says. "A specifying engineer puts his or her life on the line when recommending a process control system to run, let's say, a power plant. But no competitor was effectively or directly talking about this."

Michael developed a marketing campaign with four advertisements, news releases, compatible mailers, and brochures addressing both holes in the competitors' appeal. After the first two advertisements ran, the client pulled the campaign because it was too successful. The company had a year's worth of work and was approaching the point that it would be unable to service new business.

"The competition wall is a simple and effective approach," Michael says. "And it works for far more than merely developing advertising strategies and tactics."

A small business should be looking for competitive holes even before planning a specific campaign. By definition, a hole is something that's *not* there. What product or service is not being offered? What geographic area or demographic group is not being served? What message is not getting across? What intangibles, such as ethics, are not present in your field? One value of this approach is to help you understand your industry and market niche so well that you think of other questions about what's *not* there. Those answers will automatically flow into shaping your business and your marketing.

■ ■ ■

Tip: *When exploring holes in your market, look at competitors'
Web sites and Internet ads, print and broadcast advertising,
brochures and other marketing collateral, in-store displays,
dealer/seller training, press releases, and articles. In addition
to searching named competitors, also search the Internet for
key words that may turn up unobvious opportunities.*

6. COMMITMENT TO QUALITY PRECEDES MARKETING

Attempting to sell a flawed product or poor-quality
service will poison any marketing effort.

■ ■ ■

When Richard Karpe was a youngster learning construction, he apprenticed with a series of older craftsmen who were absolute masters at their trades. They insisted on top-quality workmanship, and Richard paid close attention. He carried that obsession for quality with him when he started own handyman and remodeling business, R. Karpe Construction, in Los Lunas, New Mexico, in 1970.

"Everything I do is top-quality craftsmanship," he says. "My slogan on my business card is 'I Use the Best. I Am the Best.' If I'm going to boast like that, I'd better be able to prove it on every job."

Perfection seems like such a quaint quality for products and services, but it is akin to ethics, honesty, and truthfulness. Any company that runs to the marketplace with flaws and half-efforts is likely to pay for that haste and imperfection with lost sales and tainted reputation for years. Major corrective action and expensive marketing might never persuade customers that the once-shoddy company is now committed to quality. In the early days, some software companies insisted that the speed of technological change forced them to market with imperfect "1.0 versions" to beat their competition. Updates, patches, and the subsequent versions were their response to complaints, and many customers put up with it because they had few or no alternatives. But increasingly sophisticated customers started shunning new products in the first year or so, pushing software engineers to do better testing and refinement before marketing.

Richard keeps a scrapbook of before and after photographs of his previous remodeling work. The cover inscription reads: The bitterness of poor quality remains long after the sweetness of low price is long forgotten. He charges relatively high prices for his time and doesn't negotiate. He has a seven-month backlog of work. Certainly, a clientele who believes Richard's promises of quality doesn't materialize overnight. It is built one project at a time. "It has taken more than 30 years to earn this stature," he says.

Attention to detail is the difference between a mechanic and an artist, Richard says. He always arrives at a job cleanly shaven, with clean shirt, pants, and shoes. He stacks his wood in perfect squares by size. He places drop cloths over all the furniture and tapes plastic over the doorway so debris doesn't go into the rest of the house. He measures three times before making a cut. He spends two hours a day keeping the project area clean.

"Everything clean and orderly about a job and personal appearance says 'I care,'" Richard explains. "I bill myself as a pro and that's what I deliver."

This commitment to quality influences your marketing plan and the type of marketing you must do. For Richard, craftsmanship *is* his marketing. He serves an exclusive clientele. Almost half of his work is with repeat customers and the rest is from referrals.

■　■　■

Which of these elements can you build into your product or service to prove its quality?

- Longer product life

- Work that does not have to be redone

- Superior ingredients

- Cleanliness

- Fast delivery

- ■ Response 24 hours a day, seven days a week

- ■ A result that works perfectly every single time, no exceptions

7. IDENTIFY YOUR STRATEGY

If your strategy is clear, everyone in the organization
will understand how he or she contributes to
make marketing successful.

■ ■ ■

Dinotown is a dinosaur theme park for family fun at Bridal Falls, British Colombia, in Canada. It is open only 100 days each year. Each spring, it starts from scratch with a new group of employees and must provide a clean, safe adventure for 3,000 visitors a day. It doesn't have time for "soft openings" and extensive staff training. The first day's visitors must experience the same great value for their dollar as those who arrive mid-season. Dinotown must have a clear, simple strategy that even new employees understand and execute. That's what Rob Ell established in the five years that he ran Dinotown for his mother, who still owns the company.

"Business owners are working strategically and tactically at the same time," Rob explains. "What most small businesses lack is a good strategy that's simple, that everyone can follow. If they get the strategy right, everything else falls into place."

A strategy defines a meaningful, compelling and supportable difference between your products or services and any alternative. All employees in a company are involved in marketing, whether they understand that role as part of their job or not. Strategic thinking and planning should make that clear. In five years at Dinotown, Rob fine-tuned the strategy so that each year's start-up was increasingly efficient and successful.

"The key principles to success are the value of your unique selling features, the caliber of your recognized reputation, and the quality of your product or services," he says. "The strategy starts at 30,000 feet and then drills down to every detail." At 30,000 feet, the owner is analyzing the opportunities and identifying the uniqueness of company, products, or services. Dinotown's defined market is kids under ten years of age—with their friends and parents in tow—who live within 100 miles of or are visiting Bridal Falls. Dinotown needs to be fun, exciting, and adventurous for kids, but also a joyful, memorable experience for their parents, Rob says. The Dinotown Web site stresses some of these benefits for visitors:

> 12 Acres of Live Shows and Unlimited Fun, Safe Rides.
> We're closer than you think at Bridal Falls, BC.
> Bring your U.S. dollar and receive a 30 percent exchange rate right at our gate.

At the detail end is the action plan listed as a sequence of activities along a time line—exactly what needs to be done and by whom to achieve opening day excellence.

Rob has been able to apply that same strategic template to countless other companies he has advised through the years. It has worked for a company that sells trampolines over the Internet and another company that sells insurance to film school students. It also continues to work for Dinotown, which has doubled in value since Rob took over operations in 1994.

■ ■ ■

Rob Ell's Strategy Steps

1. Analyze the opportunities, including defining the marketplace, what the customer identifies as strengths and weaknesses, and your unique selling features.

2. State measurable marketing objectives, such as specific goals for increasing the number of customers or average sale and planning major internal issues. Place the major focus of your marketing budget on existing customers.

3. Launch marketing strategy by pinpointing specific target markets. Identify whom and where they are.

4. Set the action plan—describing marketing tools and their roles in a monthly and annual time line—and fix the budget.

PART 2

PLAN YOUR MARKETING

■ ■ ■

Even with a firm business foundation, you're still not ready to hand out those fliers or commit to a series of advertisements. Careful planning up front will produce greater results in the end. Just as entrepreneurs resist writing a business plan, they avoid writing a marketing plan, whether for their overall company or for a specific product or service. The cost of this stubbornness is incalculable. Putting the details on paper clarifies them in your mind, which reinforces the marketing steps you need to take.

Write down your Five Ps: product (What do you really sell?), price (Are you the lowest cost, best value, or something else?), position in the marketplace (Are you the campy rebel or the tried-and-true traditionalist?), promotion (What specific marketing will you use, such as networking or ads?), and package. Whatever you decide, set goals, deadlines, budgets, and ways to measure success.

It's unlikely that one type of marketing will be sufficient for the long term. Explore the entire range available to you and select the right combination, partly based on your own style and partly on the most cost-effective for your marketing goals. The key is to plan so that you're always marketing in some way. Too many entrepreneurs market until they get busy. Then they let it slide, and eventually find that business slides too. They have to crank up the marketing machine again. This approach puts the business on a financial roller coaster that is not conducive to long-term success.

8. LET A MARKETING PLAN BE YOUR GUIDE

Successful marketing should be guided
by a carefully researched plan.

■ ■ ■

Dean Del Sesto had worked in advertising and marketing for more than two decades, but when he decided to reposition his company, Strata-Media Inc., in Orange, California, he didn't rush in with a few ads, some client phone calls, and a new slogan. He invested time and effort in a thorough marketing plan.

Many entrepreneurs know about business plans, although, unfortunately, relatively few actual write and follow one. Even fewer of them appreciate the importance of a marketing plan, either for one specific campaign or for the company's strategic, long-term direction. Marketing is supposed to turn products or services into cash. The marketing plan identifies how a company will accomplish that goal. It should make the best use of a firm's resources, unify all marketing efforts, identify new market opportunities, assign responsibilities, and set a time table for implementation. Most important, every action should be measurable. Del Sesto estimates that of those who do write a strategic marketing plan, 90 percent stick it on a shelf and 7 percent implement a few parts. "The 3 percent that execute the whole plan rule the business world," he says.

Any marketing plan starts, proceeds, and concludes with the customer and potential customer. "You must start with what the client wants, not where you want to go," Del Sesto says. "If marketing is selfish, it won't work."

In Strata-Media's case, clients wanted more results that they could measure as a return on investment. For Strata-Media to meet its own long-term goals, its marketing plan needed to address that client demand. With that mind-set, Strata-Media began developing its new marketing plan with research and plenty of it. "Research isn't rocket science. In fact, it's the simplest part," he says, "but it is the most time consuming." Such research should identify your competition; outline the who, what, when, why, and how of your market; and establish how you're going to reach that market. The information should be quantifiable, not just the fact that you're going after a big market, but that 100,000 adults within a five-mile radius buy your specific service three times a month. You can gather this information through in-person interviews with current customers, telephone and e-mail surveys, competitive intelligence, research about existing and potential customers, and focus groups.

"Every marketing plan should be about how you build an experience for the client that is different than what competitors are doing," Del Sesto says. Strata-Media determined that it would position itself as the marketing agency that delivers return on investment. Its brochure promises: Our clients will never spend more dollars with us than we make for them. Nice promise. But it must be backed up with quantifiable data. So Strata-Media points to real-life results: It generates $3 billion to $5 billion in new business opportunities for clients annually. The company couldn't make that claim if it didn't set up ways to quantify the results of its own and its clients' marketing plans, Del Sesto says. "ROI marketing is a discipline in which every tactic has a measurable result and holds someone accountable for every result."

A written marketing plan is useless if it's not implemented, he stresses, and that takes more time and effort. Strata-Media spent three years putting its new plan into action. The first year used measurable results to identify what was right and wrong with the plan. The second year worked out the bugs and added a few tactics, based on what was learned in the first year.

By the end of the third year, the marketing plan was working smoothly and producing large amounts of new business. The plan will remain useful unless the clients' mind-set changes—which was what prompted the new plan in the first place—or Strata-Media wants to reposition itself. The marketing plan has stages, he adds. It identifies some areas for future growth that the company can implement when the timing is right. No company has enough resources to do everything at once, so it should set priorities based on what clients want and need.

■ ■ ■

Tips for writing a marketing plan:

■ Do your homework first.

■ Identify what you want your plan to accomplish.

■ Commit to a tightly written effective plan, rather than a long plan that has no focus.

■ Understand what you are really selling.

■ Be honest about your opportunities and obstacles.

■ List your marketing actions.

■ Assign accountability and set deadlines.

■ Measure results.

9. MARKETING IS A COMBINATION OF MANY EFFORTS

No single marketing tactic is sufficient by itself to build your business. Use a combination of complementary tactics.

■ ■ ■

At Paul Reed Smith Guitars, located in Stevensville, Maryland, marketing is like constructing a building. One effort after another is added. Rarely is one removed. As a result, the company uses everything from personal relationships to media interviews and customer service. Most successful companies find that successful marketing depends on finding the right combination of activities and always maintaining a marketing presence, regardless of how busy or how broke they are. Founder Paul Reed Smith continually visits with customers, salespeople, and managers at dealer's locations. He takes his own managers and sales staff to dinner, drawing out in congenial conversations what each likes and wants. He emphasizes taking extraordinary care of employees and customers.

"However, if this were the only strategy being utilized, it wouldn't work," Paul says. "Also needed are product reviews, free press coverage, successful trade show executions, an effective distributor network (internationally), a valuable sales representative network (within the United States), and a core culture that includes integrity."

The company never stops modifying and improving its marketing efforts, he says. "We're always looking for at least a 50 percent success rate."

When Paul first started making guitars, he would hang out at concert arenas for seven hours before a show to make friends with musicians. These friendships led to back-stage access, where he would show his guitars to the star performers. "One night in ten, I'd make a sale," he recalls. "Carlos Santana, Al Dimeola, Howard Leese . . . agreed to check it out. If the big names didn't love the guitars, they didn't have to pay me, even when I knew I couldn't make my rent the next day."

The company never misses the two largest music retailer trade shows in the United States and one in Germany. Every other year it sends people to trade shows in other countries like England or Japan. Paul always goes in person. He spends as much as half his time on the road. "I don't sell guitars one by one anymore, but it's still personal," he explains. "I don't think people give up their money unless it's personal."

Whenever the company comes out with a new product, it makes sure every industry magazine has an opportunity to review it. Paul Reed Smith Guitars keeps a steady steam of advertising in magazines that target either dealers or customers. "We cut out magazine advertising for five months once, and it almost killed us," Paul says. Initially, he didn't want to have a Web site because of the cost and the challenge to make it interactive, but he soon found that most customers check out the company first on the Internet.

The variety of marketing efforts has built Paul Reed Smith Guitars sales to 1,800 guitars a month. Paul sees no reason to change the combination strategy. "I'll tell you what it's like. Remember the Ed Sullivan [television] show? Remember the guy spinning all the plates at one time? That's what your marketing must be like. If one of the plates drops, you're dead; you'd better get another up and spinning immediately."

■ ■ ■

Tracking Your Personal Marketing Combination:

- Keep a large calendar that lists all marketing efforts so that you can spot periods of time when no marketing is active.

- Use color coding for different activities.

- Set up a computerized list of every marketing product, quantity on hand, cost, and supplier.

- Occasionally stop a single marketing effort and carefully track any impact.

10. A DATABASE IS MARKETING GOLD

Use technology to customize marketing that will save time and money, improve communication, and get measurable results.

■ ■ ■

Ronald Stein started using contact management software even before he and wife, June, launched Principal Technical Services (PTS), a Lake Forest, California, supplemental staffing agency, in 1995. From 50 business cards, Ron has built his database of employees; existing, potential, and past customers; and job applicants to 24,000 names. He uses an off-the-shelf version of ACT contact management software.

"I was a project manager for 30 years so I expect business to be organized," Ron explains, "but it's difficult because people change jobs and phone numbers all the time. A database organizes all our contacts so nothing falls through the cracks."

A database is the most effective way to build a mail or e-mail list for multiple marketing uses. If you bought a highly targeted mailing list, it would cost at least $2 a name, but the response rate from such a list is questionable, and you can't use it repeatedly without paying again. However, people who have done business with you in the past are the most likely to become a future customer, alliance partner, or employee. A database of these people is so valuable that some companies carry it as an asset on their balance sheet. PTS provides engineers and other highly skilled technical workers for temporary assignments at thousands of client companies. Keeping in touch with that many people as well as matching available employees by specialty to specific jobs requires a computer database. The company organizes the 24,000 names into 70 different groups, such as clients, newsletter recipients, and Christmas card recipients. The software is networked among the core office staff, each of whom keeps key contacts up to date.

That database serves many marketing purposes. Ron uses it to schedule daily phone calls and meetings that keep him in touch with key customers, employees, and prospects. At the end of each call, he schedules the next time to make contact with that person—whether next week, next month, or next year—so that no one is forgotten. Ron even keeps a list of key contacts, with whom he schedules lunch on a rotating basis because he feels face-to-face meetings are so important in building relationships. More than 1,500 people receive the company electronic newsletter, which the database tracks. Each officer sends out Christmas cards to his or her own list. Whenever a new resume comes in, Ron can e-mail a personalized acknowledgment with a pitch about the benefits of working with PTS. It's vital to keep the database of workers' information current so Ron can send out market updates, which "stir the market and encourage people to update their resumes."

The database was an important part of building PTS, which ranked 143 on the *Inc.* magazine list of 500 fastest-growing privately owned companies in America in 2000. "The more we use the database, the more we figure out ways we can use it," Ron says. "Our aim is to be more efficient than our competitors. This is a very service-oriented business. We always want to stay in front of our clients."

■ ■ ■

A database can improve your marketing by:

■ Compiling and categorizing contact information about clients and others important to your business

- Allowing you to build information about a client's personal habits and past buying patterns that help you personalize future marketing contacts

- Reminding you to contact clients periodically

- Identifying your best customers and what they want

- Tracking buying preferences so you can notify a customer when favored products arrive or go on sale, or new services are added

- Spotting clients who might be in danger of becoming former clients because they haven't done business with you for an extended period

11. IDENTIFY YOUR TOP 100

Focusing on your best customers plus turning
away difficult ones will build both profitability and
your pleasure in business ownership.

■ ■ ■

Dr. Omer Reed has been a dentist for more than four decades, pioneering techniques in preventive dental care, technology, and effective business management of dental practices. Careful analysis of his own practice, Concorde Dental in Phoenix, Arizona, uncovered the fact that most of his income came from his top 100 patients, but most of his time was spent on the bottom 30 percent of his patient list.

Every business should continually work to upgrade its customer base in order to maximize successful marketing efforts and reduce owner burnout. Omer didn't identify his top 100 patients merely in terms of dollars. He factored in patients who enriched his life and made him feel happy. He asked each associate in his practice to identify the top 100 patients too. The lists were merged and not surprisingly included many of the same names. This group accounted for 85 percent of annual cash flow. Even though his and his staff's criteria were subjective, Omer next contemplated what these patients had in common and what objective criteria put them into the top 100. Some of their traits included accepting his comprehensive wellness and preventive philosophy of dental care, paying their bills, appreciating a high level of personal and technical care, and referring friends and relatives who also like quality care.

"We want to do business with people who care about themselves," he sums up.

These characteristics helped him identify his target market for future marketing efforts. Also, he learned that people tend to have friends similar to themselves, so these top patients tend to refer new patients who coincide with the desirable characteristics of the top 100. Omer and his staff compiled another list: the bottom 30 percent of the practice. Again the criteria were subjective. These were the patients who "rob you of your stomach lining and heart muscle, the joy of life and the fun of serving," he explains. He discovered that as much as 70 percent of the time in his practice was spent with the people whose names were on the second list.

These two profiles became standards against which he measured new patients who came to him. He put most of his effort into the upper two-thirds of his practice, especially the top 100. He started sending letters to the lowest 30 percent, informing them that his practice was headed into more specialized treatment so he wouldn't be able to accommodate everyone. He gave them the names of three nearby dentists. "The dentists are happy with the referrals, and these patients might not be in their lower third," Omer says.

The business owner must have self-confidence that the top two-thirds of customers will fill your time and build your business, says Omer, who has taught his strategy to hundreds of dentists and other professionals all over the world. He calls his approach the Ohana Philosophy, after the Hawaiian word for family or lasting relationship. Even businesspeople in other fields have found the strategy works wonders for their success. Omer takes his marketing strategy of the top 100/bottom 30 percent one step further. He cultivates relationships with owners of the finest men's stores, best restaurants, top-quality beauticians, and other best-of-class enterprises. He refers his patients to them and these business owners refer their customers to him. The idea is that if top patients tend to hang out with people like themselves, then owners of quality businesses will tend to have customers similar to his top 100.

The top 100/bottom 30 percent strategy "was dynamite from the beginning . . . an overwhelming, positive response from the marketplace,"

Omer says. "One must have faith to accept only people referred from this core of believers."

■　■　■

Marketing benefits of identifying your top 100:

- Spur referrals to like-minded patients

- Formalize your definition of your ideal customer

- Clarify why bad customers drain you and your business

- Achieve financial savings by not marketing to the wrong type of person

12.   MARKET WITH YOUR STRENGTHS

Every marketer has many different tools and tactics
from which to choose, so emphasize the ones that
capitalize on your style and preferences.

■　■　■

When Rachael Lewis became a coach for executives and business teams, she thought she had to market her services like so many other coaches and consultants she had observed. She joined leads groups, trade organizations, and chambers of commerce. She shook a lot of hands, inquired about each person's business and career, and hoped that someone would ask her to be his coach. "I was mildly successful, but it was painful," says Rachael, a founder of Trilogy Coaching Institute in Laguna Beach, California. "I'm an introvert. Introverts don't gain energy from being with people. It's draining. I had designed a marketing strategy that would work for an extrovert."

That comfort level is perhaps one of the biggest factors when entrepreneurs, especially solo practitioners, fail to market consistently. Some necessary marketing will take you out of your comfort zone. That must not stop you from consistent marketing. However, when you are more than uncomfortable with an unfamiliar activity and genuinely dislike the type of marketing you're doing, you will make excuses, such as "I'm too busy" or "That doesn't work." Don't indulge in such destructive behavior. You have a multitude of strategies that you can employ to market your products and services. You don't like one? Try another. You're too busy for that approach? Take another. That marketing effort didn't get results? Use another method. But don't flail aimlessly. Analyze both your business and yourself before developing a well-thought-out marketing plan that matches your personality and image—both of which are part of your brand—and that you can comfortably commit to execute over time. Even the greatest marketing campaign fails if it's not executed properly.

Rachael took the time to study before changing her marketing plans. "After taking several behavioral assessments, I looked at my natural style, attitudes, passions, and internal motivators," she says. "What would I enjoy doing regardless if it got me clients or not?"

Her expertise is in high-impact management, so Rachael started writing articles and an online newsletter, speaking to groups, and teaching workshops for business leaders. She stopped networking. Instead, she formed alliances with groups like the Professional Coaches and Mentors Association and the Professional Consultants Association whose members collaborate with her for some projects and refer clients for others.

"No more 7 AM breakfasts to shake hands and swap cards . . . unless I'm the speaker," she rejoices. She wrote a book, *Leading High Impact Teams: The Coach Approach to Peak Performance,* to further emphasize her expertise as a coach for team leaders and her ability to help them develop pragmatic remedies to obstacles and to raise their competency. "The book helps to market my business because it makes it absolutely clear what I can help clients with," she says.

She has also developed more written products because she enjoys providing resources and tools for people even if they don't eventually become coaching clients. But these materials are both marketing tools and profit centers. This introvert's approach has grown her business 25 percent. More important, marketing is easier for Rachael so she's more likely to do it consistently and with energy.

■ ■ ■

How to determine if you and your marketing technique are a bad match:

- Do you continually make excuses for why you're not marketing each day?

- Do you feel exhausted after spending some time on marketing?

- Do you find yourself doing less than your best effort during your marketing activity?

- Are you sabotaging, perhaps unconsciously, your marketing results?

13. MARKETING REQUIRES FOLLOW-UP

Most potential customers won't make a decision
based on one exposure to your marketing,
so follow-up contact is important to success.

■ ■ ■

If there is one basic about marketing that Frank Shemanski has learned since starting Southwest Financial Services in 1988, it is the necessity to reinforce every marketing endeavor with second contacts. Southwest Financial services merchant card accounts for about 100 banks. Merchant accounts are unsecured lines of credit that enable a business to accept payment by credit card. Southwest Financial verifies the creditworthiness of applicant businesses and sells or leases equipment and software to the businesses for handling electronic funds transfers and secure Internet transactions. Frank markets both to the bankers and the businesses with merchant card accounts.

"I don't like surprises, and determine my expected results before I spend any marketing money or energy," he says. "But no one's perfect, and I have been disappointed by the results on occasion. I can always trace the problem to ineffective execution of the marketing plan or lack of follow-up."

In one marketing campaign, Southwest Financial offered to 100 existing business customers personal identification number pads that are required by credit card companies. The price was low, and the customer merely had to check the appropriate response box on the form and return it. Just three replied. Frank assigned an employee to follow up with customers who hadn't responded. After two weeks, Frank found out that the employee simply ignored the assigned task. Frank insisted he make some telephone calls, which brought 10 more sales, but then he slacked off again. Needless to say the employee left, and who knows how successful that marketing effort might have been with full follow-up.

The value of following up any initial marketing effort is measurable and significant. Sales companies have found that a customer needs, on average, seven exposures to a product or service before responding. Credit card companies send out millions of mailers offering credit cards to consumers and, if fortunate, get 2 percent response, Frank says. However, if they then have their marketing staff follow up the mailer, the response rate rises, in some cases, to 20 percent. Frank prefers personal contact with his customers and referrals. But when he chooses a mail advertising campaign, he first carefully targets the recipients and sends a personalized message. Then he has employees call those recipients by telephone. "These campaigns are small and manageable for maximum success," he explains.

Follow-up can take another form at Southwest Financial, to which client banks outsource their merchant card services. Initially, when a customer opened a business account at the bank, Southwest Financial followed up later with an offer to provide merchant card services. About 20 percent signed up, Frank says. However, if the bank officer offered merchant card services at the time that the account was first opened, 80 percent signed up. So Frank continually meets with bank managers and insists that his sales representatives visit regularly with account officers to remind them to offer merchant card services. That too is follow-up.

"We have to remind them again and again, and if we don't do that for a while, [sign-ups] taper off," Frank says.

But the business owner must carefully calculate the cost of follow-up, Frank adds. On a low-margin product or service, follow-up telemarketing or visits might cost more than the profit.

"You can't afford to go back three or four times," he says. "Don't leave without answering every objection."

■　■　■

Follow up with a different means than the first contact:

- Send a letter, referring to the previous contact.

- Telephone the potential customer, and if he or she is the wrong contact, ask for the name of the correct buyer.

- Write an e-mail reminding the recipient of the first communication.

- Pay an in-person visit to the customer.

- Mail a business card, photo of the product, or a sample.

PART 3

THE BASICS

■ ■ ■

Certain aspects of marketing must be decided almost from the time you start business, and they affect your company throughout its lifetime. The name, the brand, and patents or trademarks, for example, are difficult or impossible to change later so they should be shaped with care. Other aspects are important to establish early in business, but can change over time. Location, basic sales techniques, and means of distributing products are part of marketing that evolve as your business expands. New distribution channels such as the Internet didn't exist in earlier generations, but are basic to many types of businesses now. Some aspects are so basic that entrepreneurs overlook them, such as explicitly asking a customer to buy or helping customers find your location. Still other aspects are basic to business, yet they may change with the times and the economy. Many companies adjust their pricing strategy and their approach to merchandising as their surroundings and circumstances change. The image, logo, and color are perhaps the easiest to change and sometimes should change to freshen the company's look, the way women change their skirt length and men change the width of their neckties.

Getting the basics established properly will set the tone for your company's reputation as you try different marketing campaigns through the years. The basics make it clear who you are, what you stand for, and why you're in business.

14. A PATENT-PROTECTED PRODUCT

A proprietary product is less costly to market
and commands higher profits

■ ■ ■

Light and heat destroy. That's a huge problem for museums, art galleries, and wine connoisseurs. Ruth Ellen Miller, an artist by temperament and training, and Jack V. Miller, her rocket-scientist father, teamed up in 1990 to develop lighting without ultraviolet and infrared waves for use in museums. The inspiration came when Ruth Ellen accompanied her father to a meeting of the Illuminating Engineering Society of North America, where a speaker from the Smithsonian Institution in Washington D.C. described the problems they had with fading, cracking, and splitting of historic documents caused by light. She asked her father to invent a lighting system that would work. He agreed only if she would run the company. They spent more than four years on research and development and on obtaining patents before ever taking their fiber optic lighting to market.

That very first day, the Millers received a faxed order from the Smithsonian Institution.

Their business, NoUVIR Research in Seaford, Delaware, now has 23 patents and several trademarks. Those are huge marketing advantages, says Ruth Ellen who heads the company. "You have two choices: make a generic product or a totally proprietary product without competition," she says. The first is easier and cheaper initially, but must always strive to lower its selling price. The second is hard work and great risk, but ultimately a high-profit winner if it can be produced and protected.

NoUVIR uses a projector attached to 32 acrylic fibers that terminate in a luminaire, which is a light fixture without electricity. The company has more than 50 luminaires, ranging from a pin spot that lights a postage stamp to a flood light for large displays. Its patents cover every element of the system. "Patents can be the greatest asset a company owns, or they can be worthless and a giant money pit," Ruth Ellen says. "If your patents have broad coverage and the claims—the heart of the patent—have teeth, competitors cannot imitate your product line." NoUVIR's patents are strong and the company spends money and effort on patent maintenance fees and fighting off interlopers. But the marketing benefit is tremendous.

As soon as NoUVIR's first products hit the market, large competitors started looking for ways around the patents, Ruth Ellen says. "The market is awfully lucrative. If we only had one patent, some attorney would tell [a competitor], 'sure, we can find a way around it.' But with two or three, it's more difficult. And we have 23," she says. "If our patent position had not been unbelievably strong, competition would have destroyed NoU-VIR in its first years."

Another protection is the name, which means no ultraviolet (UV) and no infrared radiation (IR). A huge competitor used the term *No IR* in its advertisements when trying to convey its fiber optic lighting as heatless. NoUVIR successfully stopped the ads on the basis that they infringed on its trademark. NoUVIR products became the lighting of choice for public displays of a 15th-century vellum copy of the Gutenberg Bible, the state of Delaware's original copy of the Bill of Rights penned in 1790, Thomas Jefferson's handwritten draft of the Declaration of Independence, two portraits of George Washington in the National Cathedral, and even a wall of $200 bottles of wines in an American restaurant. NoUVIR gets such contracts because "the lighting doesn't merely protect the objects but the balance is so good that things look right under it," Ruth Ellen says. "As an artist, I find it satisfying to walk into a museum and see our lighting."

■   ■   ■

Less than half the inventions submitted to the U.S. Patent & Trademark Office receive a patent by meeting these criteria:

1. The invention must be a machine, an article of manufacture, a process, a composition, or a new use of one of these four.

2. The invention must be useful.

3. The invention must be different from all previous inventions.

4. The invention must not be obvious to a person of ordinary technical skill.

5. If the invention is a plant, it must be duplicated by asexual reproduction.

15. BRANDING

A company's brand is more than its name. It's the whole
picture customers have of what the business does,
how it operates, and what it delivers.

■ ■ ■

John Lown had built a couple of successful companies with his ability to invent useful gadgets such as a dripless oil spout, tuna can drainers, and measuring spoons on a ring. But he wanted a home-products company for a market that was broader than folks who pour their own motor oil. As he looked through his inventions, he thought the most promising was an easy-open, airtight seal for which he had obtained both utility and design patents. Dozens of companies—some with multimillion-dollar marketing budgets—make storage containers. There seemed to be little room for a start-up on a budget. However, John's research uncovered a shortage of airtight receptacles to keep dry food fresh and to block ants that might get into the cupboard. John used his seal on some prototypes of clear plastic round jars and square boxes that one finger could open and close with a snap. Then he asked consumers what they would put in such containers. The result is a line of snap-lock storage products sold under the name Snapware in thousands of stores worldwide.

The most important marketing move for the Fullerton, California, company is "creating and building a meaningful brand that represents a clearly defined niche in the consumers' mind," John says. Snapware isn't just the name on the products, it's the image that springs into people's mind when they hear that name.

A strong brand speaks volumes about a product. Rolls Royce doesn't merely mean car, it evokes a picture of a certain type of car in a specific price range with a host of features and even an image of the personality and lifestyle of its owner. Companies that have a strong brand convey a consistent, recognizable public persona. They want that brand to be positive. However, actions speak louder than advertising words. Enron pushed its brand to mean innovation and energy, but its accounting practices and ultimate financial collapse have enshrined a different, negative brand.

That's why the inner workings of a company influence the brand. Ultimately, the brand conveys the company or product's authentic self, for good or bad.

"Branding at Snapware is all about understanding the perceived needs of our user-consumer and translating that data to a product and package that sells itself off the retail shelf," John explains. "We employ the top designers who have a passion for our niche of plastic small-box home storage solutions. Our marketing staff continually studies how consumers live and store their household items."

Snapware's first airtight containers were marketed to keep crackers and pasta fresh. With a simple label change and a dark brown top, the one-pound size became a coffee canister. Applying paw prints to the gallon size container makes it a dog biscuit holder. Adding seasonal decorations makes Snapware suitable for holiday gifts like cookies and candy. Each of these line extensions was consistent with the easy-open, stay-fresh image. But line extensions alone couldn't sustain Snapware's double-digit sales growth, so John applied the snap-shut concept to wet-food stackable receptacles that are strong enough to go from freezer to microwave and attractive enough to set on the dinner table. He named them Snap 'N Serve. Next he added larger snap-shut, stackable containers for Christmas ornaments, called Snap 'N Stack Seasonal Storage.

"Everything we develop snaps, locks, and stores," John says. That's the Snapware brand.

■ ■ ■

How to create your brand:

- Study your marketplace. What is the competition? What niche is underserved?
- Define how your company fits in the marketplace.
- Identify how you want others to describe your company. Name it before others do.
- Your brand should be a natural part of what you do, not an artificial image laid on top.

- Pinpoint the most likely customers and understand their demographics, desires, needs, and what makes them buy.
- Make sure everyone in your company understands your position in the market and buys into making the most of it rather than trying to push the business into something it's not.

16. CREATE A PROFESSIONAL CORPORATE IMAGE

Carefully choose the colors, logo, and type font to contribute to the corporate image you want to convey about your business.

■ ■ ■

A midlife reassessment drove Judy Hoyt Pettigrew to develop the concept of women's weekend retreats for sharing ideas and feelings. From that project, Judy envisioned a company for women professionals to capture contracts for work that major corporations outsource, and to help these corporations market more effectively to women, who make 82 percent of consumer buying decisions in the United States.

Judy carefully chose every element of the corporate image. Nothing was haphazard. She named the Cincinnati, Ohio, company WOW! Unlimited Inc., to convey the image of unique and energized women empowered to achieve great things. The name came from *In Search of Excellence* author Tom Peter's "wow factor." Judy explains, "We wanted our clients to say 'WOW.'"

She chose purple from the Francis Weaver poem, "When I Am an Old Woman I Shall Wear Purple." "Purple is regal and psychologists say it brings out the child in you," Judy says. "I don't know if I believe that but women realize they long to get in touch with the dream maker in them." In the company logo, the *W* in Wow! is a butterfly, symbolizing metamorphosis into something greater and better. She even gave herself the title of MOM, mentor of metamorphosis.

At its core, WOW! Unlimited is a marketing company. It promotes the skills of more than a hundred women experts. It also works with companies that want to reach the multibillion-dollar women's market. "I wanted an image that would last, that would be memorable," Judy explains. "I can't stress enough how important it is to have a clean, compelling, creative corporate image."

This corporate image or look is a significant part of conveying the company's marketing message. The colors, names, logos, and tag lines must complement and convey the message in a meaningful way. Potential clients might not even be able to explain this message in words, but they should have a clear impression about the company and what it stands for. "Everything we say, mail, leave behind on [sales] calls, or do for our clients reflects our corporate commitment to WOW people," Judy says. "It worked. Even two years after seeing it, people would say, 'we want to call those purple butterfly people.' In my follow-up calls, they would always say, 'Oh, you're the purple butterfly lady.'"

WOW! Unlimited carried through this corporate image on its Web site, using shades of purple and the butterfly throughout. "Since our mission is twofold—to help businesses that want to reach the women's market and to help women through programs, products, and services—we had to have a multipurpose site, not just an electronic brochure," Judy says. "In addition to our online corporate information, we provide direct contact information to our key WOW! women associates, a tea room and coffee shop for threaded discussions, an area to go for a little peace and quite while looking at beautiful pictures, and even an embedded market research area that is password protected for client use."

■ ■ ■

Which color conveys your corporate message?

- *Black:* power, elegance, mystery

- *Dark blue:* power, integrity, knowledge

- *Light blue:* tranquility, softness

- *Brown:* stability, masculine qualities

- *Green:* healing, restful, growth

- *Purple:* nobility, luxury, magic

- *Bright red:* vigor, leadership, courage

- *White:* purity, goodness, cleanliness

- *Yellow:* happiness, energy, joy

17. THE MEMORABLE AND APPROPRIATE NAME

The greater your ambitions for your business, the more important the right choice of its name becomes.

■ ■ ■

In 1985, Mike Carr and three colleagues started a company they named Salinon, which is the name of a mathematical symbol with four curves. "It was a terrible name for a company in the business of branding and name development," Carr acknowledges. "People couldn't remember it, couldn't spell it, and they thought it was a fish or salamander."

Within a few years the partners drifted in different directions. One kept the Salinon name with a different business, and Carr, an experienced marketing expert, needed a new corporate handle for his venture. He renamed his Austin, Texas, firm "The NameStormers," a play on words that implies what the company does, one technique it uses—brainstorming—and hints at its creativity. "What I've heard from clients is positive," Carr says. "We have secured business because they like the name, versus competitors who use their own names. Our name is easy to remember and that helps."

Some people have remembered the name for years before having a project for which they hired NameStormers. "A lot of people call and say they remembered the name and didn't know how to find us, so they searched the Internet or phone directory," Carr says.

NameStormers has the additional benefit of suggesting weather images that work for graphics and logos. Frequently, a name change for an established company is trouble. Former customers can't find it. Current customers think it was sold or went bankrupt. The renamed venture must spend time, effort, and money establishing the new moniker and that can detract from other marketing efforts.

Customers tend to dislike name changes. United Airlines spent millions of dollars trying to get the public to accept a new name, Allegis. It never caught on, and the airline finally switched back to UAL. In Carr's case, the name change didn't ruffle many feathers because the Salinon name had no value in customers' minds. If Carr intended to be a solo consultant, the name of his company wouldn't matter much, he says, because he would rely on referrals and personal contacts. But an entrepreneur that intends to grow a substantial and lasting corporation should choose the name carefully.

"The name should be memorable and differentiate you from your competitors," Carr says. "Don't focus on what you do best; focus on how you're different." Joe's Lube and Oil isn't as good a marketing tool as Jiffy Lube. Carr prefers coined phrases that imply something good about the business or product, such as Die Hard batteries.

Carr knew he had a great business name when competitors started copying it. He trademarked The NameStormers and eventually trademarked *Name Storming* as well because of copycats. "Just owning the trademark isn't enough. You have to protect it or you risk losing it," Carr says. "You have to decide whether to go after [trademark infringers] with a cease and desist letter or a lawsuit." Many entrepreneurs aspire to owning a name that is synonymous with their industry, but companies like Xerox spend millions of dollars avoiding that eventuality. Once a name is considered generic, courts won't punish copycats.

■ ■ ■

To be a valuable marketing tool, a business name should be:

■ Memorable

■ Short

■ A reflection of the image you want to project

■ Positive

■ Available as a Web URL

■ Easy to pronounce

- Suitable in other languages as globalization expands markets for even small firms

18. MERCHANDISING

Creating interesting displays of your products will allow them to catch shoppers' interest and stimulate sales.

■ ■ ■

Bob Siemon was taking a jewelry design class at a community college in 1969 when he became a Christian. He fashioned a sterling silver ring engraved "Jesus Saves" for a class assignment. The teacher called it the least imaginative piece Bob had ever made, but Christian retailers started ordering it and other jewelry and placing special orders for Christian jewelry. Bob Siemon Designs soon was selling to several hundred retailers. With an eye for both aesthetics and business, Bob realized the limitations of having his necklaces, rings, and pins laid out under a counter. Such displays are uninteresting, fail to catch shoppers' attention as they move quickly through a shop, and restrict a product from distinguishing itself. So Bob introduced to the Christian retail industry a freestanding, four-sided, pillar for displaying jewelry.

"This new system radically changed the way stores approached jewelry sales, creating departments instead of sidelines," Bob says.

Bob Siemon Designs even makes its own retail display cases and pillars, which it supplies to retailers along with the jewelry. "In the jewelry and gift industry, the most important part to selling the product is how it is merchandised," explains Dwight Robinson, marketing manager for Bob Siemon Designs. "No matter how well designed the product is, if it is not showcased or featured, it won't sell. Jewelry can literally get buried among other products if you're not careful." The company's most successful product launches are the ones that include the display racks. It allows the company to put together preconfigured packages, which makes the manufacturing, assembly, and sales projections more efficient and effective.

Merchandising is the marketing term for all the elements that feature a product at the point of purchase. The more attractively those elements are brought together, the higher the sales. Many customers will walk into a clothing store and buy an entire outfit—dress, belt, shoes, necklace, and coat—that has been creatively and prominently displayed, rather than try to cobble together a "look" by themselves. They will buy more soft drinks that have been stacked at the end of a grocery store aisle than from the middle of the aisle. They will buy more fruit that is cleaned and tidily stacked in tiered displays than piled without thought in a barrel. They also buy more Bob Siemon Designs jewelry that is neatly packaged and hanging in neat rows from hooks on a swivel tower.

Bob Siemon Designs has continually improved its display systems over the years. The company started with small displays that featured a select group of products. But the stores demanded more as the brand name became recognizable to consumers as a result of the name's prominent location at the top of the display towers and cases. As the retailers became better at merchandising their entire store, Bob Siemon Designs needed to create displays that would fit into different store styles, layouts, and designs. Sometimes the company creates customized displays to match the look and feel of specific stores. Bob Siemon Designs has been the driver of these specialized displays because he sells mostly to smaller specialty retailers. That is in the best interest of both retailer and manufacturer. "Find creative ways to display products or get lost in the crowd," Bob says.

■ ■ ■

Tips for improved merchandising:

- Observe how customers navigate through a shop in order to identify attention-catching locations for your display.

- Products displayed at eye level sell best.

- Variety in the colors you use and the size of products you group together will attract the shopper's eye.

- Lighting should focus on the merchandise.

- Keep displays neat and clean. Avoid clutter.

- Feature your company or product name prominently if branding is important.

- Group complementary products, illustrating how they work together, which will result in more customers buying the whole package of products.

19. WIN THE PRICE WAR

A small business can't survive as the low-price
leader in competition with national companies,
so it must adopt smart pricing strategies.

■ ■ ■

Pricing was something of a mystery to Michael Pata when he opened Animalmania in Ft. Lauderdale, Florida, in 1990. He used seat-of-the-pants guesswork to put a price on crickets, snakes, red ear baby turtles, and iguanas. He knew what his competitors were charging, but he also learned over the years that he couldn't get customers to think of Animalmania as the low-price leader, even when its prices were the lowest. National discount chains "weren't cheaper than we were, but they took large bags of dog food and priced it below cost as a loss leader. Customers thought everything was the lowest price as well," Mike says. "Some things are price shopped, like fish food. Customers compare our price to Wal-Mart. But when they need a fish net, they have no idea what the comparable price is."

Pricing is one of the key components of marketing. Every business struggles to charge a price that is higher than its costs—all costs—without pricing itself out of the market. The price can't be so low that customers think the product or service is low quality. The price can't be so high that customers think the product or service isn't worth it. This pricing game continues as long as the business does.

Over the years, Mike discovered that generally people shop on price for consumables but not for more unusual items, like a branch for an iguana environment. He couldn't eliminate the trial and error of pricing, but he finally bought Everest integrated management software by Icode to help him evaluate the impact of different pricing efforts more quickly so he could correct mistakes. He experimented with charging $7.99, $9.99, and $15.99 for green iguanas. Animalmania and its Web site (http://www .animals.com) sold the same number of animals regardless of price, so Mike stuck with the highest price. He sold neon cardinal fish for a dollar apiece, but found sales soared when he sold ten for $6.90. Now almost all the neon cardinal fish are sold in lots of ten. "We lose a little margin but we make more profit because we sell so much more," Mike says. He sold red ear baby turtles for $12.99 each, but dropped the price to $8 each if a customer bought three. Sales tripled.

Another pricing strategy involves giving a free hamster or parakeet if the customer buys a home environment kit for the animal. This strategy helps sell live products more quickly, which incur maintenance costs. "The software is great because I will get an idea, activate it, and see the results within a couple of days," he says. "The software automatically calculates the discounts for the Web site. Before, that was a problem because we didn't know how to explain it online."

Computer analysis also helped Mike identify errors in product deliveries. He orders 2,000 goldfish and 1,000 guppies twice a week. His inventory would indicate he had 20,000 fish on hand but his tanks were empty. So he started counting the fish, difficult as that was, which routinely uncovered shortages in deliveries. Tracking inventory and pricing on computer also allows Mike to take advantage of special discounts that sales representatives offer when they come into the store. The lower cost of product helps profitability. Continually analyzing his profits and adjusting prices quickly doubled Animalmania's profitability in two years.

■   ■   ■

Using price as a marketing tool:

■ One of the most common pricing strategies is to have the lowest price. Unfortunately, resulting buyers tend to be fickle. As soon as someone else offers a lower price, they're gone.

■ Selling below cost in an established market is an attempt to kill off all competitors.

■ A top price goes after fewer customers who are willing to pay for the best.

- A prestige price can be charged in a marketing strategy that is selling image or snob appeal.

- Bundling involves putting two or three products or services together at a cheaper price than selling each separately. This strategy helps unload a slow seller or increases perception of value.

- A buy one, get one free strategy is designed to increase the volume of sales.

- Frequent buyer programs (such as punch cards that can be redeemed for a free cup of coffee after ten previous purchases) reward loyalty.

- Price by your location. A souvenir stand at the rim of the Grand Canyon 20 miles from the nearest discount drug store can charge more for film.

20. DISTRIBUTION THAT REACHES YOUR CUSTOMERS

If you have maximized sales produced by bringing customers to you, expand your market by going to the customers through more distribution channels.

■ ■ ■

When Frank Sarris started making chocolate candy in the basement of his Canonsburg, Pennsylvania, home in 1960, he had no idea Sarris Candies would grow into a multimillion-dollar, global enterprise.

Decisions about how and where to distribute your products or services greatly impact the size of your market and the type of clientele who buy from you. Sarris Candies illustrates how these decisions changed a part-time, home-based business into a 35-employee company. It took three years to outgrow Sarris's basement, but even then he only built a small candy shop next door. Five years later, Frank demolished his house to make room for a bigger candy store. The Sarris family continued to live above the shop to preserve capital. Over the years, Sarris Candies kept expanding to a 120,000-square-foot manufacturing plant, distribution center, candy store, and old-fashioned ice cream parlor. The complex is less than a mile from Route 79 where 10,000 cars pass each hour. Busloads of senior citizens come to shop in the evening. During holidays, Sarris hires four off-duty policemen to direct traffic around the huge parking lot.

As busy as that one location is, Sarris Candies would be merely a local success story if it didn't have other means for getting its candy to people who either don't want to fight the traffic or can't make it to western Pennsylvania. A grocery store chain sent a salesman to persuade Frank to sell through other retailers. "He said, 'I'll give you 20 grocery stores.' I said 10," Frank remembers. "He said, 'let's do this right.'"

Sarris Candies went into several hundred grocery stores in Pennsylvania, Ohio, Maryland, West Virginia, New Jersey, and North Carolina. Sarris has 12 refrigerated trucks, 22 during the holiday season. Then Sarris products sold into 700 Hallmark gift shops. To accommodate such a large order without straining company delivery resources, Frank arranged to ship all Hallmark orders to one Kansas City, Missouri, distribution center from which Hallmark is responsible for sending Sarris candy to its franchisees.

"We had no intention of having our products carried in retail establishments," Frank says. It was on a special request that we initially agreed to a trial run on this endeavor. We have modified our production, equipment, and distribution to accommodate and develop this end of our business."

Another means of distribution came from Frank's son, a school teacher who wanted Sarris Candies to develop a fundraising program for his school. "By identifying the best-selling items that we produced, we put together a profitable program for schools and organizations that has enabled us to expand not only an entire department specifically for fundraising, but also a marketing program that eventually gave rise to catalog mail order and Internet ordering," Frank says. For fundraising organizations, Sarris Candies provides the full-color brochures, order sheets, and prize incentives for each salesperson, and separately boxes each order. Sarris Candies proclaims that other fundraising companies offer a higher percent of sales, but Sarris's average order is three times larger.

Mail order isn't year-round. Catalogs are available before Easter and Christmas, but those are by far the biggest times for candy sales. However, the Internet has introduced Sarris Candies to the world, not just former Pennsylvania residents hungry for a taste of home. "Surprisingly, we come to work and there are pages and pages of orders overnight," Frank says. "It's still amazing to me that people shop over the Internet."

■ ■ ■

Before opening a new line of distribution for your products or services, consider these issues:

- Will the new distribution reach new customers or cannibalize from your existing sales channel?

- What costs will the new channel bring to your company and will increased profits (not just revenues) justify the extra expenditures?

- Will you be able to maintain quality in products and services?

- How will you increase production to meet additional orders?

- Will costly incentives be necessary to attract sales in a proposed channel?

21. ASK FOR THE BUSINESS

An amazing number of entrepreneurs don't
ask for the order when selling.

■ ■ ■

Jay Furry received an unenviable assignment from his company, Century Electric Motors—take over the Florida district. Sales had dropped significantly under the previous four district managers. What had he done to deserve such a bad district? In addition, the economy was in a recession. Jay's first step was to comb through the customer files to determine the status of scheduled production. Next he looked at the correspondence that had accumulated over the previous 18 months. "I discovered many inquiries to our company that had never had a response from our company," Jay says. "I made a list of 50 companies and made them my number one priority for seeking new business."

Fortunately for Jay, Century Electric had recently launched an improved incentive plan for its distributors. One morning he walked into a ten-employee shop in Tampa that specialized in repairing electric motors for other companies. The owner hadn't ordered much from Century Electric because he received unfavorable pricing under the previous distribution plan. Jay chatted with him for about 45 minutes. "In Florida, if you don't spend half-an-hour talking about fishing, snapping-turtle trapping, what you ate for dinner, and the weather, you're dead." Then he made his presentation, ending with "I'd really appreciate if you'd give me the stock order so I can get going on this." The owner opened the middle drawer of his desk and took out two sheets of yellow, lined paper. "Here's your sign-up order. Let's go to lunch."

Jay had never had such an easy sale in his life. The order was for far more than the minimum required to participate in the new program. Over lunch, the repair-shop owner explained, "I've had a lot of presentations from guys at your company, and not one actually asked me to order anything. I was waiting to see if you'd ask. I like aggressive people who say, 'Here's what I can do for you.'"

Asking for the order doesn't have to be blunt. Jay sometimes asks, "Tell me the purchase order number and I can get this entered this morning." Jay says the "ask for the order" message was pounded into him by his first boss, who used to sell garbage disposals door to door, and by a college instructor, who was a professional salesman. "What's the worst thing the customer can do if you ask for the order? Say no. That won't kill you," Jay says. Often customers interpret the absence of a direct request to buy something or enter a service agreement as a lack of confidence in the product or service or in the seller's ability to deliver what is promised.

"Many orders are not placed because salespeople will not ask for the order," Jay says. "There seems to be some sort of feeling about being too pushy. However, asking for an order is not being pushy, but merely getting on with negotiations." Jay suggests thinking like the counter clerk at the fast-food restaurant. They know you're not in line for your health, so they ask what you want. "Boil it down to its simplest form," Jay says. "You don't think the fast-food clerk is pushy for asking, and your customers won't think you are."

■ ■ ■

Tips for breaking the ice with customers:

- Ask questions to draw out the buyer's problem that will trigger a decision to purchase.

- Shut up and listen. Don't overload the buyer with information until you know what he or she wants and needs.

- Practice. Sales techniques don't come naturally and are quickly lost if not used.

- Set daily goals.

- Develop a thick skin.

22. HOW DOES YOUR MARKETING MEASURE UP?

If you want to make the most effective and efficient use of your marketing resources, you must track the results of every effort and campaign.

■ ■ ■

Travis Crane has built OneTone Telecom Inc. of Seneca, South Carolina, from one employee to 55 and from a single location to 12 stores in three states with a simple marketing philosophy. He's willing to use any and all media, as long as they deliver customers and profits. For this philosophy to succeed, Travis establishes a budget and constantly tracks which marketing efforts work and in what measurable ways. By measuring the impact and value of each effort, he can put his money only where he gets measurable results.

OneTone sells satellite television systems, local and long-distance telephone service, cellular and paging equipment and accessories, and Internet service. "We have a computerized tracking system at point of sale, and we train employees to ask, 'How did you hear about us?' They enter the information in the computer, and I pull reports all the time," he says. He also meets quarterly with his advertising agency to analyze results and make adjustments.

"I use everything: newspapers, direct inserts, radio, television, billboards," Travis says. "For Dish Network satellite TV, inserts in the newspaper work; for cellular telephones, TV is better."

Media effectiveness varies by geographic location. In rural Georgia, radio and newspaper ads draw more effectively than television. "We find, too, that a medium can wane," he adds. "We used newspaper inserts for a couple of years, and then we noticed diminishing returns, so we hit the market with something different—billboards in specific locations." Such experiences have convinced Travis that he can't track a marketing effort once and then put it on autopilot. Success requires continual and repeated tracking. Travis doesn't track just the medium; he tracks each newspaper or billboard location. He also tracks the effectiveness of the message of each advertisement.

With his advertising agency, Travis selects specific broadcast programming when pushing a certain product. "We have a prepaid [phone] product for the credit-challenged that we advertise effectively on syndicated television shows like *Jerry Springer.* We have to use the shows that our target audience watches."

His advertising choices have sometimes been wrong. For a while, he paid to have his company name "sponsor" the sports news on a network affiliate station. Several times a day the announcer said, "Now sports brought to you by OneTone Telecom." That campaign didn't boost sales because it was just name recognition, not a statement of what the company did or a special promotion, Travis says. An effort isn't a failure if you learn from it and correct mistakes. Travis strives for "constant and never-ending improvements." To hone his tracking abilities, he moved from clipboards to computerized reports e-mailed to him daily.

"People shortchange their budget on marketing to save money, but that's a mistake," Travis says. "You have to spend money to make money."

■ ■ ■

Tips for tracking the results of a marketing effort:

■ Set goals. How will you know you've succeeded if you don't know what you're seeking?

- Set up equipment and methods to collect data by which you can measure results.

- Always ask customers where they learned about your company.

- Test a marketing effort or the wording of each ad before committing a large budget to it.

- Track the difference in profits between reaching more people versus a more targeted or motivated audience.

23. THE RIGHT LOCATION

The right location can offset flaws in business promotion,
but the wrong location can kill the best business idea.

■ ■ ■

Leslie Martin had flirted with the idea of opening a retail shop, but when she saw an advertisement to buy a collectibles shop in Old Towne Orange, California, she jumped at the chance. Unfortunately, she was too late.

The owner was already in escrow with another buyer, which wasn't surprising because Old Towne had become a popular destination shopping area for lovers of antiques and collectibles of all sorts. Nine months later, Leslie saw a For Sale sign on the same shop. The buyer hadn't been prepared for the long hours and hard work of retailing. This time, Leslie bought My Enchanted Cottage, which specializes in porcelains, furniture, tea sets, and an exclusive line of note cards for the upper-middle-income collector.

"You can't beat this location," Leslie says. Old Towne is a unique mix of historic buildings and made-to-look-old new construction in a district on the National Register of Historic Places. When the area fell on hard times as J.C. Penney and other big retailers moved to modern shopping malls, antique stores moved in and gave the neighborhood a distinctive reputation. As other Southern California suburban communities razed their downtowns, Orange protected and gentrified its shops around a central park and traffic circle, which traffic planners hate but shoppers in search of ambiance love. The city's chamber of commerce and many of the merchants have helped promote Old Towne as a destination shopping area for antiques. It's listed in regional guidebooks and enjoys wide word-of-mouth promotion among antiquers.

"They've already done a lot of marketing for me, so we get customers from all over Southern California and many tourists from out of state," Leslie says. "With so many antique and collectibles shops you'd think there'd be too much competition, but for this type of business, competition brings in my particular customer. And each store has different specialties."

However, the right location for one business might be disastrous for another. The right location for your business is a combination of proximity to customers, need for transportation, access to suppliers, availability of required support services, environmental restrictions, government regulations, and rent. Nonretailers often overlook location as an element of marketing. Entrepreneurs like Leslie realize that a lot of foot traffic, good visibility, and easy access are marketing factors. But a service business, such as a plumber, doesn't need those elements because the workers go to the customer's home or office. In that case, nearness to freeways and ample parking for vehicles are important so the plumber can assure fast service. Manufacturers also want to be near highways, railroads, or ports to easily ship their products for the lowest price, which is another important element of marketing. Professional services might seek the prestige of a high-rise office building, but an attorney who specializes in injuries may find that a ground-floor office and parking within a few feet of the door are marketing pluses. Businesses that draw only from the surrounding community need a location with enough population to support their products or services. Firms that sell only over the Internet have no such geographic limitation, but they do have location considerations related to shipping and customer service.

My Enchanted Cottage doesn't have those location considerations, but Leslie does have to be mindful of parking availability and the importance of Old Towne retaining and building on its rustic yet comfortable image as a destination shopping area. "Everyone supports each other and cooperates with other shops in the area," she says. "That's a marketing plus."

■ ■ ■

Factors to consider before selecting a location:

■ Visibility

■ Accessibility

■ Rent as a percentage of anticipated revenues

■ Parking

■ Amount and speed of passing traffic

■ Government restrictions, regulations, zoning, and signage rules

■ Flexibility for future expansion

■ Nearness of adequate customer base

■ Security for customers, staff, and inventory

24. POINT THE WAY

Make it easy for customers to find your business by
providing directions, maps, and multiple means of contact.
Don't assume customers know your location.

■ ■ ■

Cal and Rose Schoch ran a gas station on Main Street of Strouds-burg, Pennsylvania, when Rose read in a trade magazine that, in order to survive in the 1960s, service stations had to diversify. Two weeks later, a Harley-Davidson salesman stopped by and offered the Schoches a dealer-ship. That was 1966. Eleven years later, Harley-Davidson said the couple would have to build a new store or lose their franchise. They lived on a small farm in Stroudsburg near the entrance and exit of the newly extended Routes 33 and 209. That's where the Schoches built their new Harley-Davidson dealership, gas station, convenience store, and deli.

The location seemed out in the middle of nowhere and motorists were still unfamiliar with the highway extensions. Rose learned the value of helping customers find Schoch Harley-Davidson/Buell in as many different ways as she could. "If the market has to come to you, that's different from you going to the market," she says. "Today, I put a map of where my business is everywhere I can: Yellow Pages, fliers, the Web site, any literature leaving my store, no matter what." The Web site provides the address and a detailed map. It also offers directions to the store from four different reference points. Then it adds, "If you get lost, call us and we will guide you in."

Rose doesn't take her location for granted. Even Harley-Davidson enthusiasts may not know her part of eastern Pennsylvania, or they may not have a great sense of direction. She understands that every piece of marketing material should have phone numbers, addresses, and maps. The easier she can make it to find her business, the more customers will actually make the trip. "Anything that helps customers get to you, tell them. We have a correctional facility across the street. We add that if it helps someone find us," Rose says.

Some businesses don't care if customers find their location. Many service providers like interior decorators usually go to their customer's home or office. A manufacturer or distributor may rarely see customers. But a retail business can be killed by an odd or out-of-the-way location. Even locations that seem obvious to most people can be hard to find for a new resident or out-of-town visitor. Why take the chance of losing a sale when providing maps, directions, and phone numbers is simple and adds little to the price of marketing materials or advertisements? Increasingly, consumers and business buyers shop the Internet. It costs nothing to put a map on your Web site, and putting the address and phone number on every page has the additional marketing benefit of making clear that yours is a real business, not a fiction or a scam.

Even after decades in business, Rose says she never assumes customers will beat a path to her door. "Reputation is fine. People have to find out who you are," she says, "but also, they have to find you."

■ ■ ■

Simple techniques that make it easier for customers to find your business:

- Maps or written directions in all marketing materials and advertising

- Detailed directions if your location is within a building complex or office park

- A phone number with an invitation to call for directions

- Photos of your building in advertisements and on your Web site so customers will recognize the place when they arrive

25. EXPERIENCE SELLS, IGNORANCE DOESN'T

Don't undermine the experience and longevity
that differentiate you from competitors.

■ ■ ■

Brea Electric Company has been a family-owned electrical contractor in Southern California since 1932. Current owner Richard D. Holly is grandson of the company's founder, and he literally grew up in the business. His dad would take him along on work calls when Richard was a small boy. Richard started working weekends and summers in the business while still in high school. From an early age, Richard understood the marketing value of the fact that Brea Electric was not just a family-owned, local business but that its owners also had many decades of electrical contracting experience.

Any company that has built up decades of experience should capitalize on the distinction that sets it apart from most of its competitors. A study by the U.S. Small Business Administration's Office of Advocacy found that about half of businesses in this country close within five years of start-up. They aren't always failures. Some are sold. Others close because the owner pursues a different path. In good economic times, some businesses close because the owner has a better opportunity in a job with another company. So businesses that survive and thrive through three generations are rare and should trumpet that success. Richard gets the point across in several different ways. Advertisements and telephone directories state "family owned since 1932." When potential customers call, he can tell them when their home was built just by the address and can recall what type of wiring was commonly used in construction at that time that might be causing problems now.

"People respect the foundation, reputation, and long record of success," Richard says. That's especially true in fields like electrical contracting, which scares a lot of untrained homeowners.

However, one marketing effort undermined that reputation. Richard was canvassing for business door to door. It was too expensive to pay fully trained technicians $20 to $30 an hour to do this work, so Richard hired young kids to go door to door to stress the dangers of aluminum wiring and the prevention work that Brea Electric could do. For example, aluminum wiring could cause electrical receptacles to go on and off intermittently. Richard mistakenly thought the youngsters' eagerness was sufficient. It wasn't. "I learned you can't send an untrained person or someone of limited knowledge to market a repair service like that. Unless they had been in the field, they couldn't answer any questions." Needless to say, no homeowners were persuaded to sign up for this remedial work, which wasn't cheap.

Now Richard is always asking himself, "Why would I use me?" That question usually focuses his mind on ways to emphasize Brea Electric's long-time expertise in the marketplace. If some marketing effort hints that the company doesn't have the knowledge that should come with longevity, it probably won't maximize results. Richard has even found that experience and longevity in business have expanded his marketplace beyond the city limits of Brea. "People tend to think of us as their local company even if they live several cities away," he says.

■　■　■

Ways to stress experience when marketing:

- State either the number of years you have been in business or the company's founding year in advertisements.

- After the company reaches a milestone, like 10 years or 25 years in business, print that fact on stationery.

- When you reach one of those milestone years, have an open house or a special sale to spread the word.

- Develop a handout or brochure that gives tips or explains some advanced area of your industry to underscore your knowledge.

PART 4

CUSTOMER SERVICE

■ ■ ■

If you don't have customers, you don't have a business. Customers separate the professionals from the hobbyists. Entrepreneurs who want to build companies that will last and benefit society serve their customers. It's not an inconvenience, it's a fact of life.

That's why customer service is one of the foundational issues of marketing. Serve the customers and they give you money. The better you serve them, the more money they're likely to spend with your company.

Some business owners say one of their favorite parts of business is interaction with their customers, and not just because of the money. The odds are good that these business owners provide good customer service.

If customer service is so basic to business and to marketing, why is poor service one of the biggest complaints consumers have about companies with which they deal? The Golden Rule—treat others the way you want to be treated—is easier said than done. It requires translating the theory of how you want to be treated into an action list that everyone in your company follows. It requires top executives to model the right behavior. It requires hiring employees who consider it an honor, not an imposition, to please others. It requires training and reinforcement of the customer-service action list every day.

Consumers have multiple choices when spending their dollars today and increasing impatience with indifference. Successful marketers make it fun and easy to do business with their companies. Once that relationship is established, the marketer must be proactive to encourage customers to come back time after time.

26.

CAPITALIZE ON CUSTOMER DISSATISFACTION

Never underestimate the marketing value of
solving a problem that irritates customers.

■ ■ ■

Bob Warren faced a tough assignment: Push his company's product past competitors that were well entrenched in the marketplace. Although the corporate parent company was the well-known international paper manufacturer Boise Cascade Corporation of Boise, Idaho, Bob's division, Boise Paper Solutions, wasn't the leader in this particular product—carbonless paper.

Many marketers stress the importance of being first to market. That is a significant advantage in branding, product positioning, and sales. However, many pioneers lose that advantage when followers present better solutions to customers' problems at lower prices. IBM introduced the first personal computer in 1953. American Telephone and Telegraph developed fax machine technology in the 1920s. Eterpen Company in Argentina was the first to market the ballpoint pen in 1938. All surrendered their first-to-market advantage to innovative competitors.

"The basic technique is to listen to customers' needs and frustrations as compared with their expectations and offer a solution to close the gap," Bob explains.

That technique sounds simple, but it requires the marketer to see what is *not* there—the hole in the market that entrenched competitors are either ignoring or choosing not to fill. Perhaps the most difficult challenge is to listen to customers with an objective mind. Success requires you to start with the problem. Many entrepreneurs start with what they want to sell and insist that it solves the customer's objections.

Bob and his team talked with companies about how they used carbonless paper and what they wanted but weren't getting. He discovered that key potential customers for Boise's carbonless paper had two basic needs. First, they wanted a product that would produce a black copy instead of a blue-colored one, because they perceived black to be of higher quality, yet they didn't want to pay more. Second, they believed their current supplier of carbonless paper was unresponsive to their needs.

Boise Paper Products needed to deliver a new paper that produced black copies. Then the company needed to make sure it set up a system to deliver responsive, customer-friendly service on a consistent basis. Marketing that merely promises a solution but doesn't deliver it will put a company in a worse position than when it started because its brand will be perceived negatively. After delivering the product and service, Boise Paper Products still needed to convince potential customers—with branding and positioning—that both solutions were real and permanent.

"The two key objections to overcome were primarily ones of credibility," Bob says. Customers demanded assurances that Boise could sustain its pricing and responsiveness. "Some credible evidence and initial successes were required," he says. "The key was to get one anchor customer who was well respected by others in the business to make the change to our product. Then success begot success." Bob's strategy doubled Boise's sales volume of carbonless paper in two years.

The challenge of displacing a deep-rooted competitor often seems complicated and difficult. After all, inertia plays a role in customers sticking with the way they've always done something or with the product they've always bought, despite its imperfections. "The key lesson is the power that is unleashed when dissatisfied customers become aware of a credible alternative that can and will meet their needs," Bob says.

■ ■ ■

Satisfying an unhappy market:

- ■ Listen. Find out from your most likely customers what bothers them about currently available products or services.

- ■ Break down their complaints into solutions your company can actually resolve.

- ■ Your solutions must surpass, not merely match, your competitors' offerings.

- ■ Don't overpromise. Be honest.

- Never stop listening. You will bar new competitors from filling needs you have left.

27. PROVIDE VALUE TO CUSTOMERS

Flashy or elaborate systems cannot replace well-planned, practical solutions to customers' needs at reasonable prices.

■ ■ ■

When the federal General Services Administration decided to award some of its contracts in Alaska to small companies in 1994, five Anchorage men with diverse technical and marketing skills created a new company, DataFlow/Alaska Inc., to compete for some of that work. Government contracts for products concentrate on the lowest price, but for services, the buyers are looking for technical competency.

"You can price information technology services to make a killing, but we weren't going to do that," says Rob Lapham, the partner who handles marketing for the 107-employee company. "We're not about the latest technology or esoteric practices unless it is important for the mission objectives."

A customer who receives the precisely suitable result at the best value will tell others, which is a better, long-term profit strategy than charging top dollar or delivering inadequate service. So the DataFlow partners from the start articulated a mission statement to take a principle-centered, win-win approach to database design, Web site development, programming, and other IT services the company performs for others. "Business isn't a zero-sum game," Rob says. "Delivery of value to customers comes back to you. Fairly dealing with customers is the reason we continue to grow."

While DataFlow does some IT work for mid-sized private companies, 90 percent of its contracts are with federal government agencies. Buyers for different agencies know each other, Rob says. Once a company delivers quality work, practical solutions, and good design, the word spreads. "We have dozens of satisfied customers now. Any procurement officer who needs something done will check with his colleagues."

DataFlow continually gets the message across that it understands the economics of value through its monthly reviews of each contract's progress, Rob says. Before the meeting, DataFlow sends a one-page summary stating what the task is, what has been completed last month, what will be finished in the coming month, and how the IT services work to deliver needed solutions. "Sometimes these meetings are only 10 minutes, but that gives us an opportunity to find out about future contract opportunities," Rob says.

One such opportunity evolved from a 1997 meeting in which Data-Flow president John Rathjen explored whether the company could save a government agency money by automating its work. That project never materialized, but it made DataFlow executives aware of the federal government's interest in identifying and tracking fish without physical tags that can harm them. The concept was to photograph and "tag" fish using their skin spots based on pattern-recognition technology. DataFlow could provide the core technical work of enormous databases and software. The company searched four years to find fisheries scientist Paul Skvorc to handle the scientific aspects of the project called The Natural Tag, or TNT. This research-and-development project alone could increase sales sevenfold by 2010 and could be used for identification and tracking of other types of animals.

"Our IT work will continue to focus just on Alaska, and TNT will be sold all over the world, but both will be marketed with the same value ethic," Rob says.

■ ■ ■

Tips for delivering value that is the key to long-term profitability:

- Value isn't just about price. Other factors include convenience, reliability, quality, status, and relationships.

- Understand what factors of the value proposition your customer appreciates most.

- Accept that each customer prizes a different value mix and make individual adjustments.

- Value isn't delivered if the customer doesn't recognize it; so clearly convey the cherished benefits you have delivered and how the customer is better off as a result.

- Recognize that you can't be all things to all people, but strive to exceed the expected value within your targeted niche.

28. TRAIN YOUR EMPLOYEES

Employees won't deliver outstanding customer
service if you don't believe in the concept
yourself and teach it by word and action.

■ ■ ■

Customer service isn't just a promise; it's a commandment at Mitchells/Richards, which owns high-end clothing stores in Westport and Greenwich, Connecticut. Once, an executive phoned CEO Jack Mitchell in desperate need of a topcoat immediately for an important business meeting. But the store was out of the color and size the man wanted. Jack loaned the man his own topcoat, which was the perfect match, until a replacement arrived. That's the type of do-anything-to-please-the-customer service that Mitchells/Richards commands of every employee. You can tell new recruits that they're empowered to please, but if everyone from the owner down the chain of command doesn't model the expected behavior, it won't become part of the company culture.

"I'm on the [store] floor every day . . . with a tape measure around my neck to send the message that no one is so high up in the organization that they are above waiting on customers," says Jack.

And he insists that every associate spend some time on the front lines too. That includes his brother, Bill, who is Mitchells/Richards vice chairman, and their father, who started the store in 1958 and is now retired but still comes in occasionally. Jack and Bill learned customer service from their parents, who insisted that customers coming into the store ought to be treated as though they were coming into the Mitchell home. The process really begins with interviewing and hiring new associates, Jack says.

Most are experienced in retail, but the company looks for people who are competent, confident, have a positive attitude, and have a passion to be the best. The most important quality Mitchells/Richards looks for is integrity. It even gives applicants an integrity test developed by Reid Psychological Systems. "Integrity is a central element that runs through all the other attributes," Jack explains.

Jack doesn't like saying the company trains its associates. "Training is for dogs," he says. He prefers the term *educate*. Mitchells/Richards has its own "university," which is a series of tapes and seminars on such subjects as how to talk to customers and how to use a calendar to build customer relationships. "I embellish the tapes, do a little role modeling, and then we literally have all our new associates watch and listen to our veteran sellers—how they sell, how they follow up, how they put down a tie when showing it to a customer," Jack says.

Outstanding customer service is an outgrowth of a relationship between customer and sales associate, Jack says, so the company uses its computer to make sure repeat customers are assigned to a specific associate. That customer database is an important tool to help the associate remember personal facts about a customer, his clothing preferences, and how long he waits to pick up finished alterations. The highly protected database has tracked every sale at Mitchells since 1989 and at Richards since 1996. Associates learn to ask questions to build a customer's profile. The company distributes daily reports about how many profiles each associate has done. If an associate is below average in profiling, he or she works with a manager to improve this ability.This information is vital for associates to serve customers beyond their expectation every time they call or walk into the store, Jack explains.

Quality service doesn't happen by chance. A company must continually monitor associates' performance, Jack says. Mitchells/Richards keeps detailed reports on each associate's performance—not as a potential punishment tool, but as a guide for continual improvement. Every Monday the company gives each associate a personalized playbook with past sales performance and future goals, customer satisfaction reports, potential customers to contact, and other information to enhance service and performance. Often, associates gather for an informal meeting to share their stories of customer service. Customer service is a mind-set built on detail. "Eye contact is important," Jack says, "so we ask our associates if they know the color of their top customers' eyes."

Although Mitchells/Richards is extraordinarily systematic about commanding and building customer service, Jack insists that it's not supernatural. "Anyone with customers can do it."

■ ■ ■

Tips for building better customer service into your business:

- Define what customer service means for your business. Set expectations.

- Start with yourself. If the owner doesn't model excellent service, no one else in the company will either.

- Hire the right employees, looking for ones with people skills as well as technical expertise.

- Measure performance and share it with each employee.

- Continually train workers in customer service.

- Reward employees who exhibit exceptional customer service.

29. TRAIN YOUR CUSTOMERS

You can boost sales and increase loyalty if
you train customers to use your products.

■ ■ ■

After 25 years in the building maintenance industry, Larry Shideler invented a better backpack vacuum cleaner. He sold his cleaning business to launch Pro-Team Inc. in Boise, Idaho, in 1987 to make these vacuums for the professional cleaning industry. At that time, cleaning companies used what is called a zone cleaning method in which each worker cleans everything in his territory of the building. But Larry knew from years of cleaning experience that a cleaning company could save money and do a better job by training each worker for a special task. In the team cleaning approach, one person vacuums the entire building, another cleans all the restrooms, and so forth.

The owners and employees of cleaning companies—like most customers—resisted change. Their attitude was, "This is the way we've always done it." Distributors didn't like the idea either. Instead of selling a vacuum cleaner for each member of the crew, they only sold one for every four workers. "We had to go to the end users, get them excited not just about our backpack vacuums but the new cleaning approach, so they would demand the products from the distributors," Larry says.

At first, Larry went to trade associations to meet people, get invitations to visit their businesses, and see how they worked. But sales were slow. "I decided to devote an entire year to seminars to educate the business owners about backpack vacuums and team cleaning," he says. "We trained the company owners and school administrators. If change is going to happen, it has to come from the people who are going to spend the money." In the seminars, the customers tried out the backpack vacuums and discovered they were powerful, yet lightweight. They learned how team cleaning increased worker productivity as much as 30 percent. They realized they could buy less equipment. Once management was convinced, they wanted Larry to train their building supervisors, tenants, and cleaning crew.

"I didn't want to be a seminar presenter, but I had a number of requests from large companies to come in and reorganize their entire system," Larry says. "It's real time consuming." But it also boosted sales. "We took off pretty briskly after the first couple of years of training," he says. Pro-Team was profitable by 1991 and now sells tens of thousands of vacuums every year. Pro-Team, a pioneer in the backpack vacuum industry, now has more than 25 competitors but still has more than 50 percent market share.

Eventually, Larry turned the training over to others, and Pro-Team sponsors the seminars. The company provides videotapes explaining team cleaning. These videotapes need to be provided in the native language of the workers as well. But hands-on demonstrations are important too. Without adequate training, some workers are tempted to sabotage the new team cleaning process. Follow-up is crucial to make sure everyone retains the initial training in order to maximize effectiveness. If workers go back to old habits and the customer doesn't reap the full productivity increases, it's not as likely to place future orders. Pro-Team's more than 600 distributors also have become active in training their customers to do team cleaning, which is a value-added service that establishes the distributors as authority and promotes customer loyalty.

In 2003, Pro-Team introduced a line of vacuums for residential use, and education is an important part of the rollout. Without education and testimonials from other home users and consumer groups, the backpack vacuum would end up being a novelty item. "Pro-Team believes that a similar educational or awareness program will be needed in the home market for our new backpack vacuum," Larry says.

■ ■ ■

ABCs of educating customers:

Ask customers what they already know about your business, products, or services.

Be careful not to make your seminars or educational booklets too self-promotional.

Concentrate on the basics that your customers need to know to make wise buying decisions.

Do a variety of educational activities such as hands-on experience or field trips.

Encourage questions.

30. MAKE IT EASY TO PAY

You can increase the percentage of customers who buy from
you by offering many different choices for payment.

■ ■ ■

Seth Greenberg and Ken Kikkawa sell more than 55,000 products to hobbyists around the world through several Internet sites, the main one being at http://www.ehobbies.com. With a huge inventory of radio-controlled cars, toys, and games, the last thing the pair wants to do is chase buyers away by making it difficult to complete the online purchase. They streamline the online buying process, but also offer as many different options for the final step—payment—as they can. They accept credit cards; PayPal, a non-credit card online payment system; cashier's checks; money orders; and have an online layaway plan. They're even considering a loyalty reward program that allows frequent buyers to accumulate points with each purchase that can be redeemed for merchandise.

"We want to make it easy to buy from us," Seth says. "That differentiates us from other suppliers and similar Web sites."

The concept of accepting multiple means of payment is the same for brick-and-mortar businesses as well. Retailers that don't accept checks may dodge the occasional one returned for insufficient funds, but how many customers do they chase away? If enough check writers want to buy from a company, a point-of-sale check and credit card approval system is a justifiable cost of doing business and of marketing. Seth says eHobbies doesn't accept personal checks because customers don't like the lengthy wait for the checks to clear before merchandise is shipped. On the Internet, speed is of the essence even as companies and consumers try to protect themselves against fraud. But the online retailer still accepts money orders and cashier's checks if the buyer is willing to wait.

The hobby retailer accepts all four major credit cards (Visa, MasterCard, Discover, and American Express). A merchant account that enables them to accept credit cards is a must for Internet sellers because 90 percent of online purchases are paid for by credit card. For retailers with a physical location, the payment breakdown is about 42 percent cash, 29 percent check, and 29 percent credit card, but even that varies by the price tag. The higher the average sale, the more likely the buyer will use a credit card or accept the seller's buy-on-time program. Many sellers don't accept American Express because it charges merchants higher fees, but again, eHobbies doesn't want to lose sales to people who want to use their American Express card. It's a cost of doing business.

More than 30 million online shoppers have an account with PayPal, a company owned by Ebay online auction site, which enables them to quickly and securely make a non-credit card payment. So, of course, Ehobbies accepts PayPal payments. Another online payment option is Bill Me Later which offers the buyer the option to buy now and pay later. Bill Me Later conducts a quick credit check of the buyer, and if it approves, the deal goes through. Bill Me Later sends a bill, which the buyer can pay in full or in installments with interest.

"We have all these rules and security measures, such as shipping only to the billing address for a credit card," Seth says. "But if possible, we want to make that sale. It's more what the customer wants than what I want."

■ ■ ■

Helping customers across the payment finish line:

- Accept all credit cards.

- Accept checks and debit cards.

- Make use of point-of-sale credit or check verification so that you can get swift approval of payment without increasing your risk of fraud or bounced checks.

- Explore options such as layaway plans and deferred payment.

- Offer gift cards so ease of payment is extended beyond the buyer to gift recipients.

- Implement antifraud training so your employees can identify counterfeit money.

31. REMIND EXISTING CUSTOMERS

Send customers reminders when it's time to reorder.
Don't assume they will automatically remember you.

■ ■ ■

O& H Danish Bakery in Racine, Wisconsin, may be a local bakery in one of the largest Danish populations in the United States, but it's also a nationwide company, deriving half its sales through mail order. As much as 20 percent of those orders are placed over the Internet. Mail order dramatically increases around Christmas time. Getting those orders in advance is extremely helpful for planning the company's fall and holiday work schedules for 120 employees.

So in 1990, O & H started mailing out reorder letters to past mail-order customers in August and September, says Eric Olesen, who runs the family-owned company with brothers Mike and Dale. Each letter includes a list of that customer's shipments from the previous Christmas season. Almost immediately O & H experienced a significant leap in mail-order business. The reason is simple. Even if customers are completely satisfied with your company, its products, and its services, they're busy people. They have short attention spans. Your business isn't continually top-of-mind for them the way it is for you. A friendly reminder that it's time to reorder triggers their memory and, often, another order. Getting repeat business from existing customers costs a fraction of luring new customers, so reorders are important to growing a company.

"The customer almost always repeats the order and adds additional shipments," Eric says.

When O & H receives these reorders, staff can easily create the new order on computer with just a few keystrokes. That's quite a savings from treating thousands of orders essentially unchanged from year to year as if they were new. But the reorder letter generated an unexpected bonus, Eric says. "Many customers give us an additional order to 'ship now' because they can't wait for Christmas, which is still months away."

Now at Christmas time, about half of O & H's mail orders are repeat business. Of course, none of the customers would reorder if O & H didn't deliver authentic Danish Kringle and other top-quality pastries, based on old-world recipes that Eric's grandfather, Christian Olesen, brought with him when he immigrated to the United States. O & H has new facilities, yet still makes the pastries by hand using all-natural ingredients, as Christian did when he and Harvey Holtz bought a closed bakery in 1949.

The reorder reminders, common in such industries as magazine publishing, require a computer system that can generate past customer records quickly and merge the data into a simple, friendly letter. Computers can also be programmed to recognize when customers might need to reorder, based on their buying history. This reminder approach should work even better for year-round consumable product manufacturers than it does for O & H, which only uses it for Christmas orders. But it is also useful for service providers, like tax preparers and dentists. Computers may lead O & H to try another step. The brothers are considering sending the reorder reminders by e-mail to their customers that place Internet orders, but so far still use traditional mail for these customers. "There's something about getting a letter and having time to look over [the catalog] before placing the order," Eric says.

■ ■ ■

A reminder to existing customers should contain:

- A history of previous orders

- A list of *all* company products or services; don't assume even regular customers know about everything you can supply

- Several featured or new products or services that the recipient might want based on past orders

- A thank you for past business

32. CALL YOURSELF

The person who answers your company's phone is either
your best first impression or your worst marketing tool.

■ ■ ■

Occasionally, Nancy Friedman calls her own company, the Telephone Doctor in St. Louis, Missouri, just to hear how her employees treat callers. Oh, they know it's her calling, right? Wrong, she insists. She asks to speak to herself and no one has ever said, "Is that you, Nancy, just messing around?"

This is a simple technique that Nancy teaches clients during her customer-service training. But she's smart to use it on her own business. Nothing would make a customer-service company appear worse than poor customer service. The best compliment that Nancy receives from callers is, "Gee, that's the way I want my company phones to be answered." She hears it all the time.

"Not to know how your customers are being handled is a cardinal sin," Nancy says. "After 20 years of interviewing and working with thousands of large- and small-business owners, I can say with confidence that very few are satisfied with how their phones are answered."

The first hello is your business's best—or worst—marketing impact. Like that old dandruff shampoo ad said, you never get a second chance to make a first impression. Also, you'll probably never know the sales lost, customers turned off, and opportunities missed because of poor telephone skills. "The first person who answers the phone is the voice of the company," Nancy says. "If you believe that, why on earth do you let just anyone come in and grab the phone?"

Nancy started Telephone Doctor after being treated rudely by her insurance agent's employees. Over the years, she has added seminars that she presents to clients in 28 countries, and books and videotapes in seven languages. Many business owners don't even think of telephone etiquette as part of marketing, but customer surveys have found that telephone pet peeves rank high among the complaints, including rudeness, phone answerers who don't give their name or the company name, and unreturned phone calls.

Answering the telephone properly and helpfully isn't difficult. The answerer needs just three elements: a buffer, the company name, and the answerer's name, Nancy says. "Buffer words are the welcoming words that say to your caller, 'I am so glad you called.' It can be good morning, Merry Christmas, happy Tuesday," Nancy says. "Without buffer words, the name of the company is cold and uncaring." Some creative buffers are "It's a great day at XYZ Company" and "We wish you were here at the Bydawee Inn."

"The buffer slows you down a tad and allows the company name—the most important part of the greeting—to be heard," Nancy says. "And then say, 'This is Nancy,' not 'Nancy speaking.' Anything after your name erases your name. 'How can I help you' isn't necessary in the initial greeting. Your name at the end speeds the rapport-building process."

Many phone-conscious companies place mirrors in front of the people who answer the telephone. They're much more likely to smile, and a caller can hear that smile in their voice. The companies also train their employees to speak slowly and distinctly, especially when giving their name, the company name, or a telephone number.

■ ■ ■

Telephone habits that are marketing pluses:

- Record yourself or employee answering the telephone and play it back for the person involved.

- Cultivate patience and politeness, even with rude callers.

- A quite, unruffled response turns away many a wrathful caller.

- If you can't help the caller, refer him or her, even if it is to a competitor.

- Never answer the phone and say "please hold" before the caller has an opportunity to speak.

- Return phone calls promptly. If you can't, leave a voice mail message explaining that you will be away until a specified time, and give the caller the option to speak to someone else.

33. MONEY-BACK GUARANTEES

Guaranteeing your products and services not only
gives customers confidence in you, it gives you the
self-confidence to walk away from a difficult buyer.

■ ■ ■

Thomas Martin decided from the moment he opened Martin Investigative Services in Anaheim, California, that the customer would always be right. Many companies give lip service to that cliche, but this private investigator backed it up with a money-back guarantee on all his services. A guarantee or warranty is the least expensive, confidence-building marketing tool for a competently run business with quality products and services. Most people are at least a little leery doing business with an unfamiliar company, especially if it hasn't been in existence for many years. To take the risk out of the transaction and to reassure customers, promise to give them their money back if they're not completely satisfied. A guarantee builds the customer's confidence in the business, product, or service. It's usually an inexpensive tool as well, because relatively few people demand their money back if they receive quality products and services.

"The money-back guarantee proved to be a phenomenal way to attract business," Tom says. "It gave the clients a comfort level at the beginning of our relationship."

It also proved to build a comfort zone for Tom and his employees, all of whom have worked for the Federal Bureau of Investigation. The guarantee becomes a means to screen out clients who are difficult or create problems.

"You can't just pay lip service to the offer," Tom adds. "No matter how hard it is, always keep your word on the guarantee."

Tom is confident the guarantee won't be needed because of his skills as a former supervisory federal agent with the U.S. Department of Justice and his employees' FBI training and experience. While clients rarely invoke the money-back guarantee, the hardest demand to honor is from people who hire Martin Investigative Services to find a lost relative. "We find the person, but the client calls back and says, 'the guy is a drug addict' or whatever problem he might have, and [the clients] demand their money back because they don't want to have a relationship with that person," Tom says.

He once had a woman client who hired Martin Investigative Services to find out if her husband was having an affair. He wasn't, so the wife thought she shouldn't have to pay for the service. "A client like that, who's going to be a problem child, I just get her out of my hair," Tom says.

When Tom started in 1980, he assumed his business would come equally from the public, attorneys, and corporations. Now he emphasizes corporate work, partly because those emotional reasons for avoiding payment never occur. "In all these years, I've never had an unsuccessful [corporate] case, so it never comes up," Tom says. Still, Tom likes to work on individual cases where he can have a personal impact helping people with a problem. "We have to be more patient with the public," he says, "and the money-back guarantee is for our own sanity if nothing else."

■ ■ ■

Ways to assure customers that doing business with you is "risk free":

- Emphasize your competence and credentials and those of your employees.

- Follow up business transactions with a telephone call to inquire about any problems.

- Immediately correct errors and encourage employees to report them.

- Once you have a track record, stress that your product has never failed or has demonstrated double or triple the performance of its warranty.

PART 5

RELATIONSHIPS

■ ■ ■

Companies often seem like buildings and balance sheets and other inanimate objects. But business is really about and for people. The company that cannot build strong, trusting relationships won't last. One of the most valuable results of marketing is the relationships it builds with customers, suppliers, strategic partners, and even employees. All of these groups begin to see themselves as part of the team of their favorite businesses and products.

Networking is the most valuable marketing tool the entrepreneur has for building business relationships. Networking is getting to know the person as an individual and only later as a potential customer, supplier, referral source, or strategic partner if you can both benefit.

Although marketing often seems like an endless hunt for the next customer, the smart marketers realize that the most lucrative hunting grounds are right inside their existing customer lists. These are folks who are already on the team. They understand the strengths and value of a product or service. They don't have to be educated. These ongoing customers are not only the best sources of more sales, they are great resources for additional customers. If they like your company, products, or services, they're willing to tell their friends and relatives.

Many entrepreneurs are naturals when it comes to treating their customers as special individuals. Yet in an effort to be professional, some of these same business owners fail to project their own personalities through their businesses. What a mistake. Customers want to know you too.

34. RELATIONSHIP MARKETING

Building relationships requires more time and persistence
than most other forms of marketing but provides the
most successful results over the long term.

■ ■ ■

After 20 years working for a major international health care corporation, Douglas Stockdale decided in 1997 to start his own management and technical consulting firm, specializing in the life science industry. In a sense, he was building on the career he already had, only this time it would be for Stockdale Associates Inc. in Rancho Santa Margarita, California. His first marketing step was to compile a list of 50 people he had worked with or known through the various management assignments in the five divisions in which he worked for his former employer. Then he diligently added 50 more names each week until he had 500.

"In this niche, people move around," Doug says. "It's a challenge remembering all the people I've worked with and then remembering where they went. As I called around trying to find people, I would say that I was starting a consulting business and trying to find so and so. But I was also telling that person about my business. It's a very warm introduction catching up with what each [person] is doing."

Developing strong relationships is perhaps one of the most difficult but most rewarding marketing strategies in business. People do business with people they know and trust. But that trust and familiarity don't happen overnight. Most times, Doug wasn't trying to pitch anything to the people he contacted. "It was a very low-key way of staying in touch and finding out who has issues and problems," he says.

Over time his contact list grew to 2,000 people worldwide.

"This large network becomes difficult to maintain, but is necessary because I don't know when someone is going to need something," he says. "My projects are high stakes and require a lot of content knowledge."

Relationship marketing is vital in an industry where different experts are needed for specialized projects, he adds. Every Friday morning, Doug calls a dozen people to follow up on previous conversations and keep in touch. If he finds information pertinent to his work or industry, he e-mails it to 30 or 40 colleagues and clients who need it for their work. Many of these friends e-mail information back.

At regional conferences, Doug started hosting networking meetings for alumni of his previous employer. Thirty-five to 75 people attending the meeting will catch up, share information, and bring friends who are also interested in building relationships.

Doug also devotes time to reviewing his network database to decide what new services to develop so that he can leverage the relationships he has and solve issues that have become trends in segments of the industry. Although building and maintaining relationships with a multitude of clients, suppliers, friends, colleagues, and others who connect with each other to form work and personal solutions is time consuming, it is rewarding personally and professionally, Doug says. "Two or three years ago, I did an internal assessment to find out where my business was coming from. Maybe 95 percent came from my personal network or from people who knew the referral personally."

■ ■ ■

How to develop strong client relationships:

- Commit time to the long-term effort. Relationships aren't built overnight.

- Describe the characteristics, demographics, industry, and other traits of your ideal customer.

- Schedule appointments specifically for contacting clients and getting to know them better.

- Don't always try to sell something. Spend time listening and understanding.

- Keep track of conversations with clients and issues of importance to follow up in the future.

- Don't send these clients junk mail or e-mail spam. Send personal letters. Make personal phone calls.

■ Enjoy people. Don't just look at them as a job or dollar sign.

35.

THE VALUE OF
REPEAT CUSTOMERS

Repeat customers are more valuable and loyal,
yet most companies spend all their marketing
focus on attracting new customers.

■ ■ ■

Most of the work at North Wind Inc. in Idaho Falls, Idaho, comes from companies and government agencies that the environmental consulting firm has done work for in the past. That's no accident. President Sylvia Medina is continually in contact with well-established customers even if they're not currently working on a project together. "Communication and respective nurturing of relationships were fundamental aspects of my marketing success from the beginning," she says. "The effectiveness obviously increased as my reputation and recognition in the industry grew."

It is puzzling that most companies spend more time, effort, and money chasing new business than on retaining existing customers. Every study documents the value of the repeat customer. The Direct Marketing Association says that in business-to-business sales, a repeat customer spends, on average, 60 percent more than a new customer. The Harvard Business School says that service businesses that increase customer retention just 5 percent achieve a 70 percent increase in profits. Several studies have found that companies must spend five times more to attract a new customer than to win more business from an existing customer. You don't have to educate those existing customers about what your company can do for them or persuade them about the quality of your product and service. Yet two-thirds of customers who leave one company for a competitor do so because the first company treated them with indifference.

Sylvia is continually on guard to make sure that doesn't happen at North Wind, even as it has expanded to offices in 12 states. She is not only technically skilled in environmental remediation, but she's personable. She remembers details and follows up on each promise. She sends personal notes to individual customers. Most important, "our quality of service must be superior," she says. "When you do that, it's so much easier to get repeat business from a customer."

But Sylvia has found that repeat customers are more valuable to North Wind than just their own contracts. They refer their colleagues in other government agencies to her. "My continuous contact with well-established customers is key, not only to strengthen our existing relationships but also to stimulate the opportunity for new introductions," she explains.

At the same time, existing customers have proven to be challenging to the status quo at North Wind.

"Customer requests for increased resources, which were neither inclusive of the company's core competencies nor consistent with anticipated growth, forced an immediate need for additional personnel and major capital investments," Sylvia says. When such requests occur, a company must weigh whether it is better to turn down the unexpected new business or find ways to grow. Neither is necessarily wrong, but the company must retain the same high quality standards without straining resources to the point of damaging the core business. Chipping away at the foundation could chase those loyal and valuable existing customers away. In fact, it could force them away if the wrong kind of growth drives the company out of business.

"Without attention to the performance, the effort invested in establishing these relationships would be lost," Sylvia says.

■ ■ ■

Ways to retain existing customers:

- Provide superior products and services.

- Never take an existing customer for granted. Always remember that indifference could send them to a more attentive competitor.

- Suggest another product or service they might not know that you can provide.

- Communicate with customers frequently, even when there's no current project.

- Provide the best value for the price.

- Offer frequent buyer rewards.

- Give discounts on volume purchases.

- Give specials for repeat customers only.

- Thank your customers often with notes and phone calls.

- If something goes wrong with an order, fix it fast and apologize in person.

36. CULTIVATE REFERRALS

Don't merely ask for referrals. Build a systematic way to encourage satisfied customers to lead you to new business.

■ ■ ■

When financial planner Keith Offel first meets with new clients, he explains not only how he makes money for them, but also how his company, Money Concepts FPC in Fullerton, California, profits. The compensation is not all cash. "The way we are paid, in part, is with referrals. If we do a good job for you, will you give us referrals?" Keith asks each client. Most clients reflexively agree. But Keith doesn't stop with that up-front disclosure.

Referrals are among the most profitable fruits of marketing. But to obtain quality referrals requires a systematic process that involves quality work on your part, relationship building, and reminders. Keith and his staff follow up initial client meetings with a series of letters that detail what has happened to their investments, how Keith has proceeded with the promised work, and what the results have been. The final letter in the series asks for referrals. A self-addressed and stamped envelope is enclosed. Most clients come through with the names and contact information of parents, aunts, uncles, and friends who just changed jobs or received a buyout from a previous employer, as well as other people in need of financial advice.

"Seventy-two percent of our new business comes from referrals from our good clients," Keith says. "We found that it is much harder prospecting for people who don't know you than it is to ask for referrals from our best clients."

More important than the series of letters, Keith says, are the ongoing frequent contacts with clients. They receive periodic phone calls and anniversary and birthday cards that Keith signs personally. "I knew one client was having family problems. I called him on his birthday and he thanked me for the card. He said it was the only one he had received.

"We also work closely with tax professionals," Keith says. "They are very picky on who they send their clients to. But if you do a good job for your clients, they tell not only their friends, but their accountant, and he becomes a great source of new-business referrals."

Keith keeps a to-do list of people he needs to call and special occasions to acknowledge. He spends an hour each month signing cards to clients. Twice a year, he presents catered dinners with a presentation about the economy and financial investments. He also hosts client appreciation parties at which he recognizes the person who gave him the most referrals and the one who gave him the biggest referral. One year, the party was a casino night. Another was a bay cruise. "I spend a lot of money on client services," Keith says. "People like to be acknowledged."

In 1998, Keith extended his cultivation of quality referrals by creating his "Referral Club." In quarterly newsletters, he highlights the referral givers. "Everyone wants to be in the club," Keith says. "Sometimes, someone calls and says, 'you only have me down for two referrals, and I gave you three.'"

■ ■ ■

Tips for attracting business referrals:

- Fix your target first. Describe the ideal client who is most likely to benefit from your products or services.

- Make a list of qualified people you know: business colleagues, friends, family, and networking partners.

- Share with your qualified list your plans to expand business and the description of people most likely to need your help.

- When someone gives you a referral, send a note or call to say thanks.

- Follow up on every referral.

■ Reciprocate by sending qualified customers to those who refer business to you.

37. WORD OF MOUTH

Genuine word of mouth advertising is really the product of long-term marketing, not a marketing campaign itself.

■ ■ ■

Experienced event planner Kim Jorgenson bought a bakery in 1990 and converted the 1,200-square-foot shop into Plums Café & Catering in Costa Mesa, California. The concept was to be a place where everyone from plumbers to tycoons felt comfortable. Just leave the plungers and diamonds at the door. Plums quickly developed a large following, especially of weekend regulars: people who came for leisurely Saturday breakfasts of eggs benedict and mimosas (orange juice and champagne), and Sunday brunches of alderwood smoked salmon and fresh dill tomato hollandaise after church. Kim also catered events out of the small kitchen.

By 1999, she finally had to expand Plums to 4,100 square feet, but the project required Kim to close the café while she gutted and remodeled the upscale bistro. She continued catering from a temporary commercial kitchen. The eight-week remodeling stretched into eight months. Although the catering had continued, Kim was sure all her old café clientele was gone. She thought it would be like starting a new restaurant and rebuilding a reputation and client base. "[Because the remodeling] took so long, we believed our guests would have forgotten about us," Kim says.

On a Wednesday, she decided to reopen on Sunday, five days later. It was to be what's known in retailing as a "soft opening" with no publicity, so the staff could work out the kinks and routine with just a few customers. "We did absolutely no advertising or announcements about our reopen date," Kim says. "The exception was a few guests who called to see if we were open. We said we would open on Sunday, however [we asked them not to] tell anyone as we wanted to take it slow."

Kim thought she'd be fortunate to serve 75 customers that first day. Plums' doors opened and the stampede began. More than 575 customers came in five hours, almost double the bistro's previous one-day record crowd. "What puzzled me is how these people knew," she says. "As guests were waiting for their food, in some cases up to an hour, I went around and asked how they found out we were opened." Some said they drove through the parking lot every Sunday in hopes that Plums would be reopened. One regular customer said he had started a "Plums Alert" e-mail group.

The word of mouth was phenomenal, "almost as if we planned it," Kim says. But customers didn't participate in a formalized word-of-mouth marketing campaign. They spread the word as a result of Plums' continual quality service and food, and friendly atmosphere.

"Restaurants have a life. One day you're hot; the next day you're forgotten if you aren't constantly listening and delivering what customers want," Kim says. "We're always looking for ways to keep the romance alive, to bring our customers fresh roses."

Plums still has its weekend groupies, but the memory of that reopening still astounds Kim. It's the kind of marketing that money can't buy. Only time and attention buy word-of-mouth marketing.

■ ■ ■

How to encourage word-of-mouth advertising:

- Be exceptional. No one raves and recommends a mediocre product or service.

- Build relationships. Network with other business professionals.

- Broaden your horizons. Develop a diversified group of friends and fans.

- Give, give, give. Reward customers who bring their friends to your business.

- Ask for help. After you've delivered your best, ask the customers to tell their friends.

- Share and share alike. When a business gives you an outstanding experience, tell others.

38. WHAT DOES YOUR CUSTOMER THINK?

Customer surveys can tell you what business you're
really in and what your crucial selling points are.

■ ■ ■

After more than eight years in business, you'd think Lynn and Dick Seaholm would know every aspect of their business, Rich Mar Shirts and Signs in Costa Mesa, California. They have built a thriving livelihood applying personalized transfers on clothing and other products. Yet the Seaholms learned something new—the value of talking to their customers—when they sought to identify how Rich Mar differentiates itself in a competitive marketplace.

The simplest path to satisfying customers is to give them what they want, so the Seaholms wanted to identify what those desires were. They focused on the division of their company that provides lettering on uniforms for youth sports teams. They identified what *they* considered to be the most important reasons team moms chose Rich Mar for the lettering on their children's uniforms. The Seaholms thought that the convenience of one-stop shopping and competitive pricing were keys to their success. They also thought the short time between order and delivery of product, accuracy, and flexible hours were pluses. Fortunately, they didn't act on their own presumptions. Instead they asked the team moms. Even the smallest firms can use customer feedback to decide whether to introduce a new product or service, or to determine what the company's image is, where service is weak, or when to drop a particular product.

Setting up a formal, measurable process to evaluate market research is important. Many businesses print "Tell us how we're doing" on their sales slips or provide suggestion boxes at the checkout counter. But these actions are pointless unless they have a purpose for the information—marketing, employee training, use of capital resources, etc.—before seeking customer feedback. Decide how you will use the information. It will help shape the questions you ask.

The Seaholms had a third party do the phone survey, reasoning that customers would be more candid with a disinterested caller than if Dick and Lynn called personally. In addition, an outside firm is more objective and unlikely to get defensive about respondents' criticisms. The Seaholms also could have chosen mail surveys, in-person interviews, focus groups, or other methods. Phone surveys are good when you're in a hurry and the survey is short. However, Americans seem to have an allergic reaction to telephone surveys. The majority won't cooperate. In this case, the phone survey worked because the respondents had done business with Rich Mar in the past. The biggest problem with a phone survey, Dick says, was reaching people during the day. If you could find someone who would answer the telephone, they usually were willing to answer the questions.

The results were opposite of what the Seaholms had expected. The customers most valued Rich Mar's fast turnaround. They also prized its flexible hours. The Seaholms had presumed those to be near the bottom of the list of values, with quality of products at the top. "The results were quite surprising," Dick says. "Although they agreed with our original set of values, the order of importance was inverted."

Information about your customers' desires doesn't help unless you act upon it. The information can provide the basis of an entirely new marketing campaign or suggest minor modifications that bring major profits. In the Seaholms' case, it did. "In the past, we made presentations to team moms telling them what we do, not how we do it," Dick says. "Now that we knew exactly what kind of customer service they wanted, we told them that's what we do." In addition to telling team moms about the features of the uniforms and team banners, the Seaholms stressed that the uniforms would be delivered within two days of order, and team banners within four days. Then they explained that because Rich Mar is home-based, the Seaholms were available during evening hours and on weekends to handle every detail of the orders. The result? They more than doubled their orders that year.

"We learned to be specific about what customer service is," Dick says. "It must be based on what your customer really wants and not on what *you* perceive as great service."

■ ■ ■

Ways to find out what your customers think:

- Written questionnaires mailed to customers
- "How are we doing" forms available in a prominent place in the business

- Surveys handed to customers as they enter the business, with instructions to return by mail (provide the self-addressed, stamped envelope) or placed in a sealed box that assures anonymity

- Questionnaires on your Web site that allow feedback and comments via e-mail

- Telephone surveys

- Evaluation checklists given to customers at the conclusion of a project or transaction

39. SYNERGISTIC RELATIONSHIPS

Developing a special relationship with a supplier or customer requires each party to bring something to the affiliation that the other lacks.

■   ■   ■

Information Systems by Design Inc. (ISD) in Scottsdale, Arizona, didn't always have offices across the nation to integrate technology for large companies and educational institutions. Initially, President Ron Watkins struggled to develop business as a value-added reseller, unable to get the favorable pricing and service he wanted from the original equipment manufacturers. Sometimes he could get better prices from distributors than he could from the manufacturer. While low prices are essential in high technology, because profit margins are so slim, Ron couldn't get the service he wanted from distributors. So he started working to build relationships with a cadre of companies that produced the products that he liked and ISD used most. He would first engage the sales personnel, progress to the sales manager, and then move to the business development manager. Sometimes Ron needed to go all the way to the chief executive officer to form special relationships.

Over time, ISD gained a reputation with these manufacturers for making a networking solution work, regardless of the bugs and problems. "We were brought in many times when other companies just couldn't solve the problem," Ron says. "If you do this for a client, you gain trust."

Occasionally, ISD would team up with the manufacturer to try to win a contract involving a very large project. But more often, the manufacturer's sales representatives worked independently to win a contract. If a prospective client was leaning toward a competitor, ISD was then brought in to evaluate that competitor's promises or to recommend the optimal way to solve the problem. "My reputation as an independent and unbiased consultant was strong enough to have some influence," Ron says. Often, ISD's solutions became part of the winning contract.

In synergistic relationships, the sum is greater than the parts. Each company brings an essential skill or product to the task or project that others lack. Partnering and alliances are the quickest way to grow a company while reducing overhead and risk, and improving cash flow. However, you must be careful to select the right partners for the right projects so that your contribution to the big picture distinguishes you from your competitors. ISD initially tried to take on all projects for all clients in all markets. "Only by focusing on technology niches (large corporate computer networks and network security) did we successfully and consistently obtain new clients, which we retained and continued to provide additional value [to]," Ron says.

Once ISD won a new client, that company was incredibly loyal, he adds. After ISD solved the problems of one project, the client would move on to another contract or sale with different problems. The client had two choices: search for a new vendor that specialized in that problem or ask ISD to figure out how to solve it. "They would consistently ask us to provide many other services, some of which we did not have expertise in," Ron says. "We found that they were willing to let us get the job done, although in many cases we had to become experts in something totally new."

This can-do attitude forces ISD to carefully hire employees who are willing to tackle new projects and learn new skills, and remain accountable for their decisions and work. Those qualities, although difficult to teach, are more important than college degrees and certificates. The company and its employees must care more about keeping special relationships strong than about money. "The key to relationships is to give more than you get and to realize that the payback is often not direct," Ron says.

■ ■ ■

Tips for developing synergistic relationships with other companies:

■ Identify companies that will create a win-win relationship with you.

■ Give more than you expect to get. Paybacks can come in indirect ways.

■ Allow those you help to return the favor.

■ Be honest about your capabilities.

■ Be willing to learn and tackle unfamiliar problems.

40. LEVERAGED MARKETING

Small businesses with insufficient funds can maximize their marketing through relationships with companies that are already well entrenched in an industry.

■ ■ ■

When Alfred Ortiz established Source Diversified Inc. in 1987, he knew he lacked the capital to build his own brand and to win large contracts for selling and customizing computer hardware and software and for managing technical manuals. So he decided to link with prime contractors that either could not or did not want to provide his specialized services. "These major technology companies do a lot of work branding their name, which makes the phone ring," Al says. "It's very difficult and expensive for a small firm to do branding, so teaming with big companies is a great opportunity."

Al focuses his marketing on these major technology companies, rather than the end user, usually a government agency or another large corporation. By this means, he leverages his marketing dollar for his San Clemente, California, company. "If I'm successful in convincing them that we're going to enhance their sales, they will, in turn, recommend us to their customer," he adds. "When a billion-dollar supplier recommends someone to the client, there's a high level of confidence in us."

But the key is creating a high level of confidence in the major supplier so its managers would recommend Source Diversified. First Al identifies one of the dominant technology companies in his field that does not provide his customized programming or technical manuals. "Then I spend a lot of time identifying how that company's sales force is structured," he says. "I identify people, talk to people, develop relationships with salespeople, so they're comfortable opening up to me."

In one case, a major distributor of computer parts had separate sales representatives assigned to each industry, a structure that offered Source Diversified multiple marketing partners within one company. Al started at the top, calling the chief executive, who referred him to the area managers, who in turn referred him to the district managers, who referred him to the unit managers who each oversaw ten or more sales representatives. Starting at the top is the best strategy because a referral from a boss carries more weight with the employee than a referral from a subordinate. "I'd schedule a meeting with the sales team, bring a pizza, and explain our capabilities and how we would increase their sales," Al says.

He repeated the process with other major technology companies. At any point in the process, he would stop if the relationship wasn't a good match for Source Diversified. Over the years, Al has leveraged his marketing through 20 major corporations.

As part of this leveraging strategy, Al went through the rigorous process to make it on the list of contractors of the federal General Services Administration. This designation is one way Al increases Source Diversified's value to his major technology suppliers. If an agency wants to buy a product from one of Al's leverage partners, it must buy it through Source Diversified.

■　■　■

Steps for building a leverage relationship:

1. Identify a major corporation whose products or services are complementary to yours.

2. Study how that company's sales effort is structured.

3. Start at the top when making connections.

4. Seek meetings with appropriate sales staff to explain your capabilities to increase their sales.

5. Continually work to increase your value to your leverage partners so they will refer more subcontract work to you.

41. NETWORKING BUILDS RELATIONSHIPS

Networking is not hard selling. Networking patiently cultivates long-term relationships for both business and personal needs.

■ ■ ■

Ira Miller spent 32 years in what he calls "the C suite," chief executive officer, chief financial officer, and chief operating officer at General Electric, several mid-sized companies, and two start-ups. So when he started his own consulting practice in Pinehurst, North Carolina, he built clientele by networking with people he knew in business.

Networking is probably the most used word in marketing, if not the most used technique. It is the tried-and-true method of building relationships, of giving without expecting an immediate sale, and of helping others find solutions even if the solution does not involve you. In return, others do the same for you—good returns to good networkers.

Ira started with about 100 names of long-time business associates and acquaintances who would return his phone calls. "You'd think I would have huge numbers of contacts because of my many years in business, but many people had retired or died," he says. He has built his networking list to 400 people through systematic, yet simple, methods. When he talked to friends, he would ask if they knew of anyone who needed his management skills and experiences and usually received a name or two. He collected business cards from industry conferences.

"My network gradually divided itself into particular groups—some became clients, part became mentors who care about me but might not give me business, and the largest part are contacts who fall into the category of 'you never can tell,'" Ira says.

But with networking, more isn't necessarily better. "While my network has expanded dramatically over the last two years," Ira says, "all the business I am actually signing is coming from people I knew personally while in the industry. I have closed no business with referral prospects." That fact is evidence of the lengthy time networking takes to build relationships. But once developed, those relationships tend to be more loyal and productive.

"I'm working on the quality of my network," Ira says. "You really need no more than ten people whom you can sit down with eye to eye and say, 'I need someone who can help my business, and I'll do the same for you. Are you willing to do that?'"

While Ira continually cultivates new people for his network, he also works continually to maintain the relationships he already has. He calls each person, focusing on what he or she is doing or trying to accomplish in life. "I listen for where they are experiencing pain, [and] offer connections, information, and advice as appropriate," he says. "I identify their current problem. This is an opportunity to understand the business or personal impact the problem is causing. I silently identify methods, tools, and processes that could improve the situation. I keep my capabilities in front of them and follow up periodically with a new way to describe how we help our clients," he adds.

Then Ira sets the time for the next call, depending on what was discussed. If he has asked for referrals, he will call within two to three weeks. If the person has a specific need, he actually sets the date he will call back.

Networking rarely comes naturally. Everyone improves techniques with experience. Ira says he initially went into enormous detail about how his consulting process works. Now he doesn't even discuss details until after a client accepts a proposal. "I just share that there is a way to remove the pain." Initially, he discussed pricing up front, but that focused the conversation on price, not value. "I now get the client to quantify the financial benefit of eliminating the problem," Ira says. "If you can ask three or four key questions about volume, pricing, margins, and cost, you can come up with a rough calculation that the client will agree to right on the phone."

Recently, Ira was able to boost a client's profit $8 million a year. "I will not pursue a problem that does not have an identified financial benefit since we have no way to determine if the consulting cost is reasonable," he says.

■ ■ ■

Tips for effective networking:

- Network in informal settings as well as in formal groups.

- Networking is relationship building, not hard selling. Little selling actually occurs at networking events.

- Seek ways to help the other person's pain before trying to get him or her to solve your pain.

- Shy people make good networkers because they tend to be good listeners.

- It's better to have one or two in-depth conversations while networking than to collect the business card of everyone in the room.

42. TESTIMONIALS: VALIDATION FROM YOUR CUSTOMERS

Third-party endorsements carry more weight with potential customers than your own claims.

■ ■ ■

"Your product tastes like licking a pine tree while eating liniment." "Your product tastes like skunk cooked in a rubber pot." Normally, a company would cringe at such customer comments, but not W. K. Buckley Ltd., of Toronto, Canada. Such comments are almost always accompanied with praise about how the foul-flavored Buckley's Mixture effectively stops coughs.

Thus, the company's slogan: It tastes awful. And it works.

For decades, Buckley's has used consumer testimonials in its advertising and now on its Web site to persuade new users to overcome their aversion to the cough syrup's taste because it will stop their cough.

Buckley's Mixture was first concocted in 1919 by William Knapp Buckley, a pharmacist who blended some natural ingredients to create a unique and effective cough remedy. W.K. was a natural salesman, says his son Frank Buckley. Rather than ignore the mixture's taste or try to mask it, the company promoted it. Such an approach wouldn't work if the product didn't.

"One time I had a cough so bad that I could not even talk without hacking," wrote an Ohio trucker. Then a fellow trucker from Ontario gave him some Buckley's. "My sore throat felt better, then my lungs opened up and my nose even tingled. This wasn't diesel fuel . . . just the best cough medicine in the world."

Such specific testimonials are more valuable than vague generalities. There's nothing wrong with asking satisfied customers for a testimonial. Some firms use surveys or questionnaires to elicit comments that can be used as testimonials. Just be sure customers understand how their comments will be used. Always select truthful comments. Avoid puffery and hyperbole.

Buckley Ltd., as a health product manufacturer, has another hurdle to overcome in using testimonials. "We have to be careful in using testimonials because the government is leary about a company making medical claims for its products," Frank Buckley says.

"We receive hundreds of letters a year from all over," Frank Buckley says, "about how pleased they are with the product, and how Grandma used it and never had a cough. You can say that. You just can't quote consumers saying Buckley's cured a cough because they're not experts."

Such testimonials are especially helpful for a 15-employee firm like Buckley Ltd., which competes with consumer-product giants with multi-million-dollar ad budgets. "People look at testimonials and assess their believability, rather than something a professional copywriter would write," Frank Buckley says. "The consumer decides, 'This is someone I believe and if it works for them, maybe it will work for me too.'"

■ ■ ■

Checklist for testimonials:

■ Is your product or service worthy of customer praise?

■ When customers write or speak favorable comments, do you ask permission to use their statements as testimonials?

■ Do you select only truthful statements for testimonials?

■ Do you match testimonials that are relevant to the interests and needs of the target audience?

■ In how many different marketing tools—brochures, letters, ads, Web site—do you use testimonials?

43. PROMOTE YOUR PEOPLE

The competence and professionalism of the
people in a company are greater marketing
tools than any paid advertisement.

■ ■ ■

On one level, Bioanalytical Systems Inc. (BASi) in West Lafayette, Indiana, makes and sells medical testing equipment and contract services to the pharmaceutical industry. But what BASi really sells is the knowledge of its more than 40 degreed professional employees. "Having the greatest product will not get the job done," says Dr. Peter Kissinger, chairman and chief executive of BASi. "We 'sell' our people. That, then, creates confidence in our products and services."

Its equipment and services collect the data that have proven to the U.S. Food and Drug Administration that new drugs like Viagra and Zyprexa are safe and effective. BASi has also worked with pharmaceutical researchers on AIDS, cancer, and heart disease.

The value of showcasing the strengths of your staff cannot be overstated for a technology company that sells to doctors and other PhDs. But merely stating in your advertisements or brochures or on Web sites that employees are smart and have advanced college degrees doesn't automatically convince other smart professionals with advanced college degrees. So BASi encourages its staff to be visible in trade groups, publish articles in professional journals, give lectures at scientific meetings, and step out as industry opinion leaders. These articles will never make *People* magazine. They have titles like "Increased Assay Robustness and Throughput Using Automated 96-Well Solid Phase Extraction" and "Application of Microdialysis to In Vitro Metabolism Studies."

Peter, who founded BASi in the 1970s, sets the example, having published 225 technical articles and serving on the editorial boards of a dozen journals. "Technical journals seek articles sent in by scientists and engineers [that are] peer reviewed," Peter explains. "They will not accept 'puff pieces' but serious work.

"The best way to interest scientists we sell to is to be recognized in their serious publications [including] *Journal of Neurochemistry, Journal of Pharmaceutical Science,* and *Journal of the American Medical Association,*" Peter says, because these publications are known as sources of top-quality information, which extends to the authors of the articles.

As another means to highlight the quality staff at BASi, the company developed its own respected quarterly journal in 1983, entitled *Current Separations,* which is even carried in public libraries. BASi customers submit some of the articles. The print version is mailed free to about 10,000 qualified professionals who request to be on the mailing list. The company also posts the journal on the Internet at http://www.currentseparations.com, which saves BASi postage to its international colleagues and customers.

The meetings of professional and scientific groups are excellent marketing venues too. BASi staff members propose titles or abstracts and, if approved by the event's organizing committee, give presentations that make them among the most visible people at the meeting. "In general, when selling to high-level professionals, being a participant is ten times more powerful per dollar spent than any advertising, perhaps a hundred times," Peter says.

The same strategy works in many other industries from accounting to engineering, he believes. "Sitting home and sending e-mails will not get the job done. A better mouse trap is not enough," he says. "People buy from people they know and trust or about whom another professional says, 'this gal can be trusted; her product works great.' You've got to be a player."

■   ■   ■

How to enhance the visibility of you and your staff experts:

■ Write articles for recognized trade journals and newsletters. Most will give biographical and contact information for authors.

■ Develop a company publication with quality information.

■ Speak at meetings or sit on panels during conventions.

■ Apply for grants, awards, and other recognition for staff work.

■ Post staff work and awards on the company Web site.

■ Encourage employees to be active and seek office in trade groups. Pay their dues and expenses if possible.

44. INFLUENTIAL RELATIONSHIPS BUILD CREDIBILITY

Don't underestimate the marketing value of a well-known client,
but you still must deliver quality products and services.

■   ■   ■

Holly Safford ran a modest catering business, The Catered Affair, in Hingham, Massachusetts, when Michael Dukakis ran for governor in 1982. Holly was a Democrat and Dukakis fan from his previous stint in the governor's chair four years earlier. She wrote a two-paragraph letter to the Dukakis campaign offering her support as a voter and her services as a caterer if the campaign scheduled any events in the South Shore area south of Boston. The letter itself wasn't very professional, she acknowledges. It didn't have a letterhead. She handwrote her name and return address. Yet a campaign representative called and set up an interview to find out how Holly would cater a dessert and coffee event for about 40 people in an elegant private home.

"I felt tremendous anxiety during that whole meeting," Holly remembers. "The woman was very impressive and wanted me to give visuals. I didn't have any. I had to describe my vision."

The dessert party was a great success, so Dukakis used The Catered Affair exclusively for these smaller campaign events in private homes. These events took her out of her modest suburban area and into high-dollar markets. They also brought favorable press coverage and exposed The Catered Affair's work to corporations and individuals who have provided a steady stream of work since.

"No one took us seriously until then, and we parleyed [the work we did for Dukakis] into a lot of great corporate relationships," Holly says.

Dukakis was elected and used The Catered Affair for his inauguration events and for the swearing in ceremonies for each of his appointees. For the next eight years as governor and presidential candidate, Dukakis used The Catered Affair for many of his gubernatorial dinners and parties. "We did whatever they needed at the price they needed," Holly says. "Sometimes we would serve lunch for four people in his office and then do a reception for 600 people the same day."

Many small businesses, especially in their early years, seek out celebrity or well-known corporate clients. While such relationships can provide a major marketing boost, as Holly discovered, they can stretch a business's resources. A corporate client may demand more time and resources than the small firm can provide. Other business opportunities may suffer.

The important key to The Catered Affair's success with Dukakis and other accounts, Holly says, is delivering quality work and producing successful events. "They knew they could count on us. We made their life easy," she says. The Dukakis events "gave us more credibility and great exposure, but to fail to perform would kill us."

The Catered Affair has grown to 350 full-time and part-time employees. It has three divisions: catering for corporations, weddings, and special private events; the restaurant at the Peabody-Essex Museum in Salem; and kosher foods for Jewish events. *Boston Magazine* named the company "Best Wedding Caterer" twice.

■ ■ ■

Caution: One value of working with celebrities is to use them in marketing materials. However, many of these clients will not allow their names to be used in marketing materials. Be careful to obtain permission before promoting your past work with such clients or future projects will dry up.

45. MAKE THE HUMAN CONNECTION

Never forget that potential customers are human.
Allowing your own personality to shine through your
business is a powerful plus in marketing.

■ ■ ■

As a woman in a technical field, Cristi Cristich might be tempted to strip all evidence of emotion and personality from her company, Cristek Interconnects Inc. in Anaheim, California. The company, started at the request of several major customers in 1985, manufactures electronic connectors for the military and communications industries where most of the executives and buyers are no-nonsense men.

A feminine touch might be construed as unserious and unprofessional. But Cristi didn't buy into that notion. In 1986, she bought a golden retriever whom she named Spuds. It seemed natural to her to bring him to work with her every day. "Customers—most of them from big and somewhat formal companies—would come to the office. They loved Spuds and the fact that I had my dog at work," Cristi says. These customers would send Spuds Christmas cards and bring him toys or his favorite doggie treats whenever they called.

Spuds loved to have his photograph taken. Cristi's favorite photo is of Spuds with one eye closed as though he is winking. She published it in the company catalog and on the Web site. "Whenever I would call on customers they would comment, 'You are the one with the dog on the catalog. Let me tell you about my dog,'" Cristi says. "People would tell me that they could tell I was nice and that they would get personal attention because I had my dog at work and in company literature."

Few business people would consider a golden retriever to be a marketing tool, and neither did Cristi. She just liked having Spuds around. However, most business is based on relationships and trust that build up as buyers and sellers get to know each other as people rather than purchase orders and invoices. People have pets and families and hobbies. When business executives share that side of their lives with their customers, it strengthens the human connection.

Infusing business with human touches doesn't go unchallenged. When Cristek had grown to about 100 employees, it was selected for a million-dollar contract with a huge international corporation, which sent a team to inspect Cristek's ability to do the work. "The visit was supposed to be a formality, but during the middle of my formal presentation, one of the team members said that he was appalled that his company was entrusting this business to such a small place and that he had serious reservations," Cristi recalls. Everyone, especially Cristi could feel the tension. The fate of the contract was suddenly uncertain. As the group toured the Cristek buildings, Cristi took Spuds along for some exercise. She caught up with her critic to try to persuade him of her company's competence. "He noticed Spuds, and suddenly all else was forgotten," Cristi says. "He fell in love with Spuds and began to tell me about every dog he had ever had in his life."

Cristek got the contract.

Spuds died in 2000, and Cristi now has two Labrador retrievers, Sonny and Lucca. The doubtful buyer continues to be a tough watchdog over Cristek's work, and he never hesitates to call Cristi directly whenever he has a concern. "But he has always been fair and a good advocate of the company," she says.

"And he insists on being kept up to date on Sonny and Lucca."

■   ■   ■

Connecting with the human side of your customers:

- *Decor.* Allow yourself and your employees to keep photos of family, friends, and pets.

- *Hobbies.* Display at your work samples of your handicrafts or other objects that occupy your leisure time.

- *Faces.* Place customers' photos in the company newsletter and on a bulletin board in a public place within your company.

- *Animals.* Permit employees and customers' animals at your business if they don't pose health or safety risks.

PART 6

THE INTERNET

. . .

Nothing has impacted marketing as quickly and completely as the Internet. The World Wide Web didn't even exist in 1990. Now companies can't afford not to have a presence there. The use and abuse of the Internet has moved quickly like everything else involving this technology. E-mail has gone from a novelty to a major annoyance called *spam*. Web sites have evolved from electronic brochures to dancing animation that takes so long to load that visitors give up in disgust. Online ads have devolved into popup ads that infuriate Web site visitors.

But the Internet is also a huge plus in marketing, selling, building community with your customers and employees, and reshaping the way the world does business. So ignore it at your peril. Not too long ago, a local retailer or a small-time accountant could do without an Internet presence. Increasingly, consumers consider a business without a Web site to be a scam. As more business owners establish a Web presence, they expand their businesses. The local retailer learns to sell around the globe. The accountant develops ways to work with client information and even keep the books over the Internet.

But the Internet hasn't just transformed commerce. It has transformed communication. Marketers develop their own letter writing campaigns, electronic magazines, and Weblogs to keep in touch with current customers and reach new ones. Companies learn to make it easy to do business with them 24 hours a day, seven days a week, which was never economically feasible in the old economy.

46.   A WEB SITE
IS A MUST

Web sites are the business cards of the 21st century. Many
customers, vendors, and strategic partners won't take you
seriously without one.

■ ■ ■

Brad Lustick, a former chiropractor, started a retail store in Houston, Texas, to sell back-care and other ergonomic products and to share knowledge about alleviating back pain and increasing comfort. The store wasn't exactly setting the world on fire. In 1994, Brad read a book about selling over the Internet through something new, the World Wide Web. Brad's company, originally called Comfort Etc. and later changed to Back Be Nimble, was one of the first 100 companies attempting to sell from a Web site. The Web site really started making money when Netscape introduced secure data transmission in 1995.

Back Be Nimble started with 95 products on a site hosted on another company's server in an online shopping mall. Now, the company has its own server and offers more than 1,000 products, which Brad calls "the most comprehensive catalog of ergonomic and therapeutic products available." The products range from mattresses and chairs to back supports and exercise books. "We have kept making major improvements from 1994," Brad says. "One thing we have always done is provide very complete and detailed product information that is probably superior to an actual salesperson. We added articles [such as common back pain misunderstandings and common causes of neck pain] in 1994."

The Internet has exploded since 1994 and businesses of all sizes almost need to have a Web site today, Brad says, "because people don't think you're a real business if you don't have a Web site." But this explosion has given birth to new online features such as Flash and animation, graphics, and movie clips that can slow a site down. Web sites today must avoid being so enamored with technology and design that they drive visitors away. Also, now that the Internet novelty has worn off, companies must make sure that their content is interesting, well written, credibility enhancing, and suitable for search engines, through which most people find Web sites.

"Don't go into a Web site thinking it is a less expensive way to start a business. It's not," Brad says. "Much like a brick-and-mortar store, it is simply another avenue" for selling your products. Back Be Nimble still has its brick-and-mortar store near Rice University and the Texas Medical Center, but most of the company's sales are through the Web site. Brad strives to make the site an accurate and consistent source of information about its products, which has earned it high customer review ratings from such comparison-shopping Web sites as BizRate.com and BestBuysOn TheNet.com. Brad has not sought out or paid for such ratings, he says. Those sites found Back Be Nimble.

Web sites that want sales must keep up with new services that make it ever easier to do business. If Back Be Nimble had not changed from its 1994 beginnings, it probably wouldn't be a moneymaker today. The Web site accepts credit cards and PayPal, and offers a toll-free phone number and e-mail inquiry and technical support. In general, bargain shopping on the Internet has made e-commerce tougher than it was in the early years, Brad says. "Unfortunately, customers are often gathering information on products from us and then buying from someone selling the product for almost zero profit that won't really be around to service them later. Customers used to be more interested in buying from a reputable source. They are now moving in a more price-conscious direction."

■   ■   ■

The basic features each business Web site should contain:

■ Complete contact information, including telephone number and street address

■ The name of the company on every page—visitors who come through search engines do not start with the home page

■ Fast-loading pages

■ Clean, uncluttered design

■ Compelling, understandable copy that stresses the benefits for the customer

■ Informative articles that establish your competence and credibility

- A page about the company—people like to know with whom they're doing business

- Interaction

- A frequently asked questions page

- Testimonials, case studies, and awards won

47. FIND PROFITS ON THE INTERNET

A company must capitalize on the Internet's ability
to create efficiencies for fragmented markets in
order to make money on e-commerce.

■ ■ ■

Imagine a large manufacturer of automobile parts that wants to liquidate some excess inventory by selling it to one wholesaler, not thousands of individual end users. The auction attracts 1,700 would-be buyers who bid back and forth 47,000 times over several days. Such a spectacle is virtually impossible in the real world but a common occurrence in cyberspace.

"One of the hallmarks of the Internet is creating efficiencies in a fragmented market," explains Bill Angrick, chief executive of Liquidity Services Inc. and Liquidation.com, a Washington D.C. online auction company that sells returned and surplus merchandise for retailers, manufacturers, and even the federal government.

Liquidation.com handles 15,000 transactions like the automobile parts auction each month, a tiny slice of a $100 billion industry that used to rely on a few bidders from a local area meeting in the parking lot of some industrial center. The Internet has become a major source of merchandise for the secondary retail industry including some national and international chains. The public perception is that no one makes money on the Internet except the folks building Web sites. The most visible example of this is the number of now-defunct Internet companies that advertised on the National Football League's Super Bowl one year; of the 17 Web-based companies that advertised that year, 13 filed for bankruptcy within several months. Yet many companies like Liquidation.com are alive and profitable because they use the Internet as the means to market, rather than the end. "Initially people thought they could build sales just by putting up a Web site and adding some advertising," Bill says. "In hindsight, that was very naive."

More than a thousand business-to-business Internet companies sprang up in the late 1990s. Only a handful, including Liquidation.com, survived. "We're a service business, not a technology company, just as American Express [and] General Electric are business services companies," Bill says. "We're experts in online marketing and merchandising." For customers seeking to sell unwanted goods, Liquidation.com not only offers an online auction marketplace, it warehouses the merchandise, which frees up space for customers. Liquidation.com separates the products into lots that are easier to sell for the highest prices. It combines marketing services with a conventional sales force. It calculates sales tax and generates online invoices. For buyers, Liquidation.com offers online capabilities so they can search the total inventory by type of product, condition of merchandise, value, and geographic location of the goods.

In other words, Liquidation.com isn't just marketing its auction services, it's using Internet capabilities to make a fragmented industry more user friendly and efficient for buyers and sellers. Instead of local transactions, these sales involve buyers and sellers in 80 different countries. "Our customers are businesses, so cycle time is very important for extracting the most value and using best practices in selling even surplus merchandise," Bill says. It's also important for Internet companies to use their technology to document data that differentiates them to customers, Bill adds. For example, Liquidation.com can document sales that brought revenues that were 200 percent higher than traditional auctions of similar goods.

"Business success is not just about the Internet," Bill says. "That's like saying it's all about the fax machine. It's what you do with those tools that makes the difference."

The market will reward companies that can figure out ways to use the Internet to benefit customers, not those that just set up a storefront and sit back and wait for customers to stumble in. "If you can't convey enough value to your customers that they are willing to pay for, you won't be successful, Internet or not," Bill says.

■ ■ ■

Successful methods of conducting Internet business:

- Effectively matching needs with solutions in a timely way

- Packaging products or services in a form unavailable elsewhere

- Providing higher value than competitors

- Offering greater efficiencies than alternative means of distribution

- Facilitating easy transactions

- Standing behind the sale and accepting returns unless otherwise made clear at the time of transaction

- Conducting solid business practices off-line

- Paying attention to detail and customer service

48. MARKETING WITH E-MAIL

It's unrealistic to expect customers to remember
you without continual reminders.

■ ■ ■

Till Kahrs taught communications skills to corporate executives and their staffs throughout the 1990s, and continually telephoned or mailed letters and promotions to remind past clients of his services. But as the millennium approached, Till decided to conduct his stay-in-touch marketing through the Internet. "Since we're basically an Internet business anyway, it was time," he says of his company, PublicSpeakingSkills.com, with offices in Irvine, California; Chester Springs, Pennsylvania; and Wolfsburg, Germany. The company provides public seminars and on-site training in sales, presentations, consumer service, telephone skills, business writing, and media relations.

"E-mail is a wonderfully easy, inexpensive, and quick way to stay in touch with everybody," he says.

Till sent letters to contacts, friends, and families letting them know he was getting rid of his "snail mail" operation and starting a quarterly e-mail about communications skills. If they wanted to receive this information, they had to send Till their e-mail addresses. He also mentions the opportunity to sign up for the e-mail updates during his seminars and corporate training sessions. He always stresses with his clients and friends that he never sells his lists to anyone. That assurance, he says, is vital to getting most people to sign up. Several thousand have given their e-mail addresses in order to receive Till's presentation advice four times a year. The advice might be about negotiating skills, persuasive PowerPoint presentations, or how to communicate effectively with customers.

"I keep in touch with anybody who communicates with me," Till says. "We automatically put people on the list if they've contacted us, even if they do not ultimately book a seminar with us." He also makes it easy for recipients to remove their name from his mailing list.

The quarterly e-mail "is a friendly reminder—'Oh yeah, these guys teach communication skills seminars,'" Till says. "Perhaps they moved to a different company or maybe they just plain weren't thinking about it and now they are again."

Initially, Till's tips were a couple of pages long. Now he keeps the e-mail to one or two paragraphs. "Smart business, since folks get so many more e-mails than they really need including, of course, spam," he says. He doesn't send his information as an attachment because many people, afraid of viruses, won't open attachments.

These quarterly e-mails are a continual source of business for PublicSpeakingSkills.com. The only downside is the necessity to be consistent about spending approximately 90 minutes each quarter writing and sending the e-mail, regardless of how busy PublicSpeakingSkills.com is. "I dread it," Till confesses. "However, when the receipts come in, my pain and suffering are soon forgotten."

■   ■   ■

Tips for effective e-mail marketing:

■ Use multiple ways to obtain the e-mail address of customers and potential customers.

■ Allow recipients to remove themselves from your e-mail list.

■ Never sell your e-mail list, and make sure your recipients know that.

■ Keep it short.

■ Make sure the information you send is valuable and useful.

■ Remind recipients who you are and what your products or services can do for them.

■ Determine the best interval between e-mails: too infrequent and customers will forget about you; too frequent and they become annoyed.

49. E-ZINES INFORM AND SELL

A free e-mail newsletter or electronic magazine can multiply
your revenues by giving a little information away.

■   ■   ■

Ralph Wilson was a pioneer on the World Wide Web, when he launched Wilson Internet Services of Rocklin, California, as a one-man business in 1995. Even in the beginning of teaching others how to market and make money with Internet businesses, Ralph gave away valuable information through e-books during his seminars. Later he added free subscription electronic newsletters, or e-zines, at his Web site. "My most successful marketing strategy has been developing a content-based newsletter on my industry in which I can promote my own products and services over and over again to a targeted audience," Ralph says. *Web Marketing Today* was his first e-zine, sent monthly to more than 120,000 people worldwide. *Doctor Ebiz* is a weekly e-zine with more than 66,000 subscribers and is published on hundreds of other Web sites. He also publishes a paid subscription newsletter, *Web Commerce Today.*

"I was fortunate to be on the ground floor of a period of Internet growth that, for a while, doubled the number of users every six months. It was incredible," Ralph says. "I've tried to learn rapidly and share what I've learned with my subscribers."

An ordained American Baptist minister, Ralph gives God the credit for putting him in the right place at the right time to serve others while making a living.

Ralph's e-zines are chock-full of current and useful information for small business owners trying to succeed online. Many of the articles would print out to three to nine pages or more in length. At least 70 percent of the content of each edition is articles and other informative content and 30 percent is promotions of his upcoming seminars around the country and his books, plus several two-line advertisements paid for by other e-commerce Web sites. "Content is primary. If you don't have excellent, unique content, you won't get the traffic necessary to attract advertisers," Ralph says.

His Web site makes e-zine subscription simple. He encourages subscribers to forward the e-zines to friends, and at the bottom of each mailing, he encourages any nonsubscriber recipient to sign up for future editions. A two-step sign-up process may be advisable. First the Web site visitors subscribe to the free e-zine, and second, they must respond to an automatic e-mail confirmation message to activate the subscription. This process avoids any misunderstanding about unwanted e-mails.

When Ralph sends e-zines, the subject line contains the name of the subscriber as well as "Dr.Ebiz" and the intriguing subjects of that edition. The person's name in the subject line increases the open rate 50 percent, he says. Ralph has to continually work to get his e-zines around spam filters, so naturally, he has included what he learned in articles for his publications and seminars. *Dr. Ebiz* and *Web Marketing Today* both have simple formats, also helpful in getting through the filters. While some e-zines are created in PDF format, many people don't install the Adobe Acrobat Reader required to read it, even though Acrobat is free, Ralph says. As Internet use, e-mail, and spam have increased, it has become more difficult to get new subscribers to an e-zine, Ralph says. Keeping subscribers requires top-quality information they can't get from a million other Web sites and e-zines.

■ ■ ■

Tips for building business with an e-zine:

- Provide enough content to position you as an industry expert.

- Write in a chatty tone.

- Although most of the e-zine content should be articles and other information, most subscribers will accept some promotions about products and services related to the subject matter.

- Make it easy to subscribe with just an e-mail address, but also try to collect other information about your subscribers that will help you know what interests them.

- Archive past e-zines on your Web site.

- Sans serif fonts such as Arial and Verdana are more readable on computer screens than fancy script.

- Make it easy for subscribers to forward your newsletter to friends.

50. EBAY AS A DISTRIBUTION CHANNEL

The Internet's largest auction site can be a useful means for distribution that doesn't trample other non-Internet distributors and retailers.

■ ■ ■

When Paul Fletcher and Garry Heath were laid off from an Internet retailer in 2001, they didn't miss a beat. They turned their education and experience in computers, e-commerce, and supply-chain management to a problem they had previously identified: Large manufacturers have a lot of perfectly good obsolete and returned merchandise. Most of these manufacturers lack the staff to test the returned products for defects, repackage them, and resell the goods for a decent price. Many manufacturers ship the merchandise by the boatload to other countries for ten cents on the dollar.

Paul and Garry reasoned, Why not sell it on eBay? "E-commerce success is about driving traffic to your Web site. eBay has 50 million registered users," Paul says. "It has one of the best supply-chain management tools in the world." Once considered a marketplace for individuals with unwanted stuff in their attic, eBay attracts tens of thousands of full-time businesses and even many major corporations. It's too big a marketplace to ignore, reaching millions of buyers for minimal cost.

Paul and Garry established DealTree Inc. and DealTree.com to sell technology products for manufacturers that either didn't have in-house capabilities to do it or didn't want to anger their other wholesalers and retailers. DealTree does the time-consuming work of breaking pallet loads of merchandise into individual units, testing, photographing, writing compelling descriptions, and posting thousands of products for sale on eBay using proprietary software. DealTree even handles the credit card processing and eBay fees and shipping.

Some manufacturers sign up with DealTree after trying to handle eBay auctions themselves. "They don't realize the time and effort involved," Paul says. DealTree is definitely not Aunt Tilly unloading her Avon bottle collection. It handles as many as 7,000 auctions simultaneously. Rather than spending a lot of marketing time and money trying to drive traffic to Deal-Tree's own Web site, "we let eBay drive all the traffic to our site," Paul says.

Critics say that eBay buyers only want low price, but the key to success for businesses using eBay is to establish high feedback ratings. eBay allows every customer to rate a seller's performance. Paul describes it as having every single person he ever did business with sitting on the front porch. "We provide terms that are helpful in getting positive feedback, such as a good return policy. We stand behind our products and provide technical assistance after the sale," Paul says. Technical assistance reduced DealTree's returns from 5 percent to 1.5 percent of sales, an important profit factor. After its first two years of eBay selling, DealTree had 24,000 more positive comments than negative ones. That feedback rating is a great marketing tool on eBay, giving DealTree credibility that is published for the whole world to see. Another key to success on eBay is a quality e-commerce experience with great communication and accurate descriptions of the products and their condition. "Merchandising" the site with good photos and links on every page to other similar products in your inventory is also important, Paul says.

■ ■ ■

Tips for eBay PowerSellers:

- To qualify as a PowerSeller, you must meet both quantity and quality standards so treat your e-commerce customers well.

- Run a professional e-commerce operation in every aspect of business.

- Adopt a fair return policy.

- Be mindful that eBay encourages all its users to treat others the way they want to be treated.

- Good customer service is essential.

- Establish a niche. Don't try to sell all things to all people.

- Set up reliable and swift inventory management, fulfillment, and follow-up.

- Write compelling auction ads.

- Consider using fee-based services like eBay Listing Upgrades to increase sales.

---

51. OPTIMIZE YOUR WEB SITE FOR SEARCH ENGINES

Merely submitting your Web site to search engines and
directories won't make it stand out on the Internet because
of overwhelming competition for attention.

■ ■ ■

Connie Kadansky had been a professional speaker and sales trainer for more than four years when she set up a Web site. But quickly she realized that the mere existence of a Web site, while essential in the 21st century, was not enough. As the president of Exceptional Sales Performance, in Phoenix, Arizona, she realized she needed to tweak her site to get the highest possible ranking when potential clients searched the Internet for sales trainers. A high ranking in search engine results can increase traffic to a Web site as much as 90 percent.

There's a difference between submitting your Web site to the search engines and optimizing it for search engines. The first is registering to play the game. The second, called *search engine optimization* or SEO, improves your odds of winning. A high search result listing isn't based on pleasing you; it's pleasing the search engines. Many Web site owners sign up with dozens of search engines. More than 90 percent of searchers use Google, Yahoo!, AOL, or MSN to search the World Wide Web, so many site owners limit their submissions to these four. Search engine optimization, if done correctly, will get your site a higher listing in a search result. If your site is not on the first page, which is about ten results, the chances drop dramatically that the searcher will actually visit your site. Here again, Google is the 800-pound gorilla among search engines, so many site owners are satisfied if they can please Google's "crawler," the software program that automatically searches sites to index them.

Connie could have done the optimization of her Web site herself. While optimization isn't mysterious or difficult, it's part art and part science. So Connie chose to leave this time-consuming task to an expert. A cottage industry of SEO experts has sprung up to follow search engines' ever-changing criteria for their clients. "Web designers can sabotage their clients' Web sites if they don't understand search optimization," Connie says. "You can have a gorgeous site that no one is visiting."

Search engines look for keywords in the coding on a Web site and meta tags that identify various parts of each page. Selecting the keywords that your most-likely customers will use when searching the Internet for the products and services you sell is the key to success. There's no marketing purpose in being first in keywords for which no one searches. Connie wants to be found by companies and sales professionals who need sales training. She wants to help sellers overcome sales call reluctance and fear. She wants to help sellers improve their results. Such phrases work their way into her Web site content and meta tags. Each page's title, which can be up to 80 characters in length at the top of the page, is a significant component in optimizing the page for search engines. The page's description, which most search engines display in results to tell the searcher what the page contains, is also important. This description should be a compelling call to visit the page. But if the title and description don't match the copy on the page, some search engines will throw the page out of its database.

Because the Internet has grown so vast, search engines increasingly look for Web sites of significance, as determined by other Web sites that point to or link to these sites. But link popularity isn't just a numbers game. Links at high-traffic sites are most beneficial in receiving higher ranking in search results.

Although Connie uses a search engine optimization service, she still tracks her traffic statistics every day. If she's not ranking high on search results and getting sufficient visits to her Web site as a result, she knows its time to work with her service to improve the site for better results.

■   ■   ■

Tips for getting more attention through search engines:

- Brainstorm the words those ideal customers are most likely to use when searching for products or services like yours.

- View the competition and analyze the keywords they use.

- Make a list of ten keywords that are relevant to the content of your Web site.

- Avoid poison words, such as obscenities, that cause search engines automatically to throw out your site.

- Craft a compelling description of your Web site.

- Keep the home page simple. Avoid slow-loading graphics and drop-down menus.

- Build links with other relevant sites.

- If your Web site doesn't have much HTML code, the site will be invisible to most search engine crawlers.

52.

PAY PER CLICK
CAN PAY OFF

Increasingly, Web sites find it necessary to pay
for search engine results and advertising in order
to attract actual buyers to visit.

■ ■ ■

One of the first decisions Warren Hoffnung made after creating software that makes customized candy wrappers was that his business, MyWrapper.com, would be a Web-based business. He wouldn't even try to go after sometimes costly placement on shelves in retail stores. But after creating an e-commerce Web site and submitting and optimizing MyWrapper.com for the search engines, he still wasn't satisfied with the amount of traffic and sales his site generated. That's when he turned to buying advertisements on the search engines. All the major search engines with significant traffic accept paid listings. The most popular are Google, Overture, and AOL. For example, if someone uses Google to search for "candy wrapper software" 17,000 sites turn up. On the right side of the page are six to ten sponsored links, including MyWrapper.com.

These pay-per-click or pay-per-performance ads work on keywords—Google calls them AdWords—that the advertisers buy. If Warren bids five cents for "candy wrapper software" and a competitor bids four cents, MyWrapper.com appears first on the results page. Each advertiser sets a daily spending limit.

Within the first month of launching the pay-per-click campaign, MyWrapper.com sales tripled. The value to Warren, who was on the typically tight marketing budget of a start-up, was that he only paid if a visitor actually clicked on his ad to go to MyWrapper.com. The goal of the marketer is not to get thousands of click-throughs, but to attract an actual buyer with each click-through. However, Google does reward with higher or more frequent placement the ads that get the most click-throughs. "The trick in the old days was to use the word *free* in your click-through ad," Warren says. "But ka-ching, ka-ching, you were paying 25 cents each time and the cost per sale is too high. I'd rather get the right people to click through."

So before signing up to pay for specific keywords, Warren researched the phrases customers were most likely to use to find his product. He compiled his own list, but also asked people who had already bought the software. His keywords include *candy bar wrapper, shower favors, personalized party favors,* and *chocolate paper.* About half of Warren's customers are in business to make customized candy wrappers for schools, corporations, clubs, and organizations for awards or fundraisers. The cost to buy a keyword might be a few cents—if few advertisers want that word—up to several dollars. Competition is fierce for words like *candy,* but not for *candy wrapper software.* Besides, a more generic term will attract many people who aren't interested in making their own wrappers for wedding or baby birth announcements, school fund-raisers, or birthday parties.

Warren continually reviews his keyword list, weeding out those that don't attract buyers. He has managed to drop his cost per sale by 40 percent through this winnowing process and always strives to reduce it even more. "I absolutely recommend using a professional Internet marketing firm to help with pay-per-click advertising," Warren says. "I have my core competencies and it's a matter of best use of my time. My company gives timely reports, suggests improvements for my Web site, and charges a commission on sales only. If pay-per-click doesn't work, they don't get paid."

■ ■ ■

Tips for improving the effectiveness of pay-per-click advertising:

- Show your search engine advertisement more often by increasing the maximum you will spend each day.

- Improve an advertisement's position or ranking by increasing the maximum amount you will pay per click or, on Google, increasing the number of viewers who click through on your ad and visit your site.

- Attract more search engine visitors to click through by refining the keywords you buy, creating compelling ads, or linking to pages on your site with the most relevant content.

- Refine keywords by adding more specific terms, such as *candy wrapper software,* not just *candy.*

53.

DOES GOOGLE MAKE ADSENSE?

When you accept advertisements on your Web site, consider
the value to your customers of relevant and useful ads, not
merely the potential revenue to you.

■ ■ ■

Robert Hoskins publishes 16 online magazines through his company, Broadband Wireless Exchange Inc. in Gilbert, Arizona. They all provide information to the highly targeted wireless communication industry. He gets more than 6.5 million hits from more than 110,000 unique visitors each month. He is able to attract that traffic with quality content. That level of traffic is valuable to him in his efforts to make money through the magazines by selling advertising.

The Internet went through a phase of popup and banner advertising with which advertisers became disenchanted because they didn't result in many click-throughs to the advertiser's e-commerce sites or in many sales. Many Web sites and search engines started charging for ads only when a visitor clicked on the ad (see Chapter 52). Then search engines like Google added another feature, placing these pay-per-click ads on Web sites that are mostly content driven, like Broadband Wireless Exchange's online magazines.

Google calls its program AdSense. Robert has structured his magazines with slots for eight ads along the right column on each page. He sells some of his own advertising space and uses the rest for Google AdSense. Google envisioned its pay-per-click advertising, called AdWords, to attract e-commerce sites and new sites trying to build traffic. Robert used AdSense initially to help build traffic to BBWExchange.com. Google thought the most likely customers for AdSense would be sites that have a lot of content, especially small companies that don't have sophisticated ad-selling capabilities. "Google can reach many more advertisers than I can, including companies I don't even know about," Robert says.

Robert makes more money from the ads he sells himself, but he has to spend more time and effort finding them. With Google AdSense, he spends five minutes setting up the program, and then Google's crawlers continually check his pages to match them with its AdWords advertisers. Robert uses filters so that his competitors' ads don't appear on his Web sites. "We don't want to send people to competitors because we also sell on our site," he explains. But there are still plenty of noncompeting advertisers on the Internet, such as sellers of used PBX telephone equipment, antennas, or amplifiers.

Both the advertisers and Robert have an interest in the subject of the ads being relevant to the visitors to his online magazines. The advertiser won't make any money if the visitors aren't likely customers for the products or services, and Robert doesn't want to alienate and annoy his subscribers. Both advertisers and owners of content Web sites need to carefully monitor this relevance matching. The relationship won't be much of a revenue generator for either if people don't click through on these ads in greater numbers than they have on banners and popup ads, which many have abandoned as ineffective.

AdSense is worth several thousand dollars each month to Robert. It works well because he has such heavy traffic and a well-defined, Internet-savvy niche. For Robert, Google AdSense is an effective and efficient way to provide valuable information to his visitors while he concentrates on his core competency of setting up content Web sites.

■　■　■

Maximize the benefits of ads on your Web site for your visitors:

- Create clear themes for each Web page and create high-quality information on the page.

- Monitor ads from secondary sources to assure that ads and page content match.

- If ads and page content don't match, discuss the problem with the ad provider (such as Google) about ways to modify pages for more relevant matching.

- Don't allow your quest for more advertising revenue to diminish content on your site.

- Work to attract more qualified traffic to your site.

- Don't put so much advertising on your site that visitors feel bombarded and abused.

54.   MARKET YOUR WEB SITE OFF-LINE

People spend far more time off-line than online,
so don't ignore non-Internet marketing efforts
when trying to build online traffic and sales.

■ ■ ■

After selling a financial services business in New Jersey in 1995, Bob Leduc semi-retired and moved to Las Vegas, Nevada. Initially, he did financial planning and marketing consulting. He also wrote three marketing manuals and started selling them over the Internet at BobLeduc.com. He uses all the standard online marketing tools, from writing for e-zines to getting listed by search engines. But much of his traffic is generated by a simple, old-fashioned direct marketing tool. He mails out hundreds of personalized postcards.

Many e-commerce businesses stick to the Internet to market their products and services sold through their Web sites. But customers spend a great deal of time away from their computers, so off-line marketing just makes sense. Bob had discovered the effectiveness of postcard marketing by accident when searching for faster, less expensive, more effective ways to generate sales leads for his financial services business. "I learned by trial and error how to generate two to three times the usual response from postcards for about half of the usual costs associated with using them," Bob says. If postcards worked for a brick-and-mortar business, why wouldn't they work for an online business?

Many people don't even open mail in envelopes that look like advertising, Bob says, but they're curious enough at least to look at both sides of a postcard, so they see the marketing message. Postcards work so well for Bob that one of the manuals he sells online is *Postcard Marketing*, which he has updated multiple times. The postcards give recipients several ways to contact him including the Web site, e-mail, a telephone number, and a mailing address. The last gets insignificant response but is useful in projecting the image of a real business rather than a fly-by-night scam.

Initially, Bob directed potential customers to his e-mail address rather than the Web site because he hadn't set up any way to respond to people who visited the Web site. He now offers a free online newsletter and free marketing course for which customers sign up with their e-mail address. When Bob first started sending postcards for his business marketing manuals, he rented mailing lists from similar but noncompetitive companies and publications whose readers were interested in marketing information. Now he uses his own list of past customers and prospects. If someone has bought something from him in the past, they are much more likely to buy more products from him. Anyone who has requested information within the previous 18 months receives a postcard every two months until Bob is convinced the recipient won't buy. Most new customers need five or more exposures to your name and product information before buying, so marketers have more danger of giving up too soon than in continuing to market to the nonresponsive prospect too long. "I didn't expect this traditional marketing tool to be effective at promoting Web site traffic," Bob confesses. "But it proved so effective that it has become my primary tool for generating online sales activity."

■ ■ ■

Ways to promote your Web site off-line:

- Print your Web address on your business card, company letterhead, postcards, Rolodex cards, order forms, invoices, and purchases orders.

- Put your Web address on your standard store or office sign.

- List your Web site in classified ads, commercials, telephone directory advertisements, and other print advertising.

- On voice mail and answering machine recordings direct callers to your Web site where they can receive immediate information and assistance even when your business is closed.

- When giving speeches, always mention your Web site.

- In every mailing, including bills and greeting cards, insert a sticker with your Web address on it.

- Whenever you write articles for publication, include your Web address as part of your signature.

55.

BLOG YOUR MARKETING MESSAGE

A Weblog can help a business build and
strengthen relationships and collaborations
through an interactive, online community.

■   ■   ■

Ernest E. Svenson is a respected partner of New Orleans, Louisiana,
law firm Gordon, Arata, McCollam, Duplantis, Eagan LLP. His unsmiling
photograph on the company Web site befits his background as a member
of the National Moot Court team and former clerk to a federal judge. He's
also "Ernie the Attorney." Do a search on Google for the term and you'll
reach his Weblog, or *blog* for short.

Ernie started blogging in March 2002, not so much as an intentional
marketing strategy but as a way to give personality to basic legal information. He also offers leads to good New Orleans restaurants, his experience
switching to Apple's operating system, and his Amazon.com wish list. "To
me it's nothing more than a Web site that's easy to update, making it possible for people to communicate outside the formal organization," Ernie says.

Blogs started as personal online journals often associated with teen-
age girls. But they quickly moved into the political opinion arena and then
into business uses. A blog is a frequently updated, online journal reflect-
ing the writer's personal observations laced with generous links to other
online information. Entrepreneurs realized the potential for promoting
their products and services, getting feedback from customers, developing
relationships with suppliers and strategic partners, and enlivening internal
communications. "I get e-mails all the time from people who have legal
problems," Ernie says. "Blogging is a way for a potential client to get to
know me, instead of meeting in a formal setting and chatting over drinks.
In that way, it is a marketing tool."

He doesn't actively promote his blog. However, word gets around. "I
was at a reunion for the judge I clerked for, and one of the other clerks mentioned that I blog. The other guy had no idea what that was," Ernie recalls.
"I didn't even know the URL, so I said, 'just [search] Google [for] Ernie
the Attorney.'"

Blogging has exploded onto the business scene, so a number of companies have developed ever-more sophisticated software that can turn a business blog into an information management system. You can answer customers' questions, report updates about products and services, ask for input from users, establish a secure section for employees or collaborators, and link to other sites with information about your company. The frequent updates to a blog can elevate it in search engine results, which may attract new customers who previously didn't know your business or services existed.

While the blog helps humanize your company, it can also create image problems if you don't manage employee blogs that may contradict the corporate image or brand envisioned in your overall marketing plan. You may have to use employment contracts to control what employees say in blogs in order to avoid such conflicts and to block revelation of trade secrets.

Ernie doesn't envision his 40-partner law firm starting a corporate blog, but does see the marketing benefits for a wide range of businesses from sandwich shops to a one-person law practice. "You can easily update information for your customers online," he says. "And for those who do, it's a major sign that you 'get it' about innovation and new technology."

■ ■ ■

Ways to market with a blog:

- Personalize your image with customers

- Give frequent updates about new product and service offerings

- Provide a forum to elicit honest customer opinions about your company, products, and services

- Test a new marketing message, new product, or an advertisement

- Drive traffic to other company Web sites

- Help customers find your products off-line by linking to retailers' Web sites

- Develop wider public recognition of you and your employees as industry experts, whose blog comments may be picked up or linked by other blogs

PART 7

KEEP IN TOUCH

. . .

Marketing isn't just theory. It's not pretty brochures and clever ads. You have to reach out and touch people with your marketing. The challenge—and the fun—is figuring out how many different ways you can keep in touch with prospects and customers. Businesses use letters, e-mail, telephone calls, catalogs, newsletters, and more. In fact, some businesses have so overused these methods of communications that consumers and lawmakers want to make them stop, which makes it harder on every business trying to stay in touch.

Still, you must not be shy about communicating with your market. Some business owners think that, of course, their customers know who they are and what they sell. These owners get busy and let communications slide. Is this shyness or fear? Nobody said marketing would be easy always or become your favorite pastime. If you find yourself cleaning out your storage cabinet for the second time instead of calling a few prospects, you're hurting your business. The key to keeping in touch without annoying customers is to get permission to communicate when you have information of interest and value to them. E-mail has instituted a method that other forms of communication should employ. Include a sentence at the end of a sales letter or at the back of a newsletter or catalog that allows recipients to remove themselves from your mail list. Honor all such requests. The other half of staying in touch with customers is to make it easy for them to communicate with you. Always be sensitive to the fact that if you don't keep communications open with your customers, competitors will.

56.   REGULAR MAILINGS KEEP YOU IN FRONT OF CUSTOMERS

If your company's name and products aren't regularly placed in front of people who have bought from you in the past, they will forget about you.

■ ■ ■

It's pretty hard to miss Jack Panzarella's products. His company, StreetGlow Inc. in Wayne, New Jersey, is the world's leading seller of neon and performance lighting for cars and trucks. The products were featured in the motion pictures *The Fast and the Furious* and its sequel *2 Fast 2 Furious,* and StreetGlow even licensed the movie name as the brand for one product line. In all, StreetGlow manufactures and markets 1,500 different lighting products under the StreetGlow, Fast and Furious, and OPTX names.

Still, Jack doesn't want to take any chances that customers will forget about StreetGlow. So he sends out mailings every month to 6,000 customers who have bought StreetGlow products in the past. "If you're out of sight, you're out of mind," he explains. "Talk about anything. Just keep your name in front of people."

Jack started the mailings shortly after launching the company in 1991. At first, he sent monthly postcards. Such mailings must be quick and easy to read, not too much information, he says. A postcard doesn't take any effort to open, so most people will flip the card over to see what it says. Existing customers recognized the company name and products instantly. In fact, one of StreetGlow's most successful mailers in terms of sales generated was a postcard that accidently went out without the company phone number on it. "But I have yet to send another mailer with no phone number. I just can't do it," Jack laughs.

Later, Jack changed his mailings to 11-by-17-inch pages double folded. They cost more than postcards, but the same as a regular letter and can include more information. Some mailings are about one specific product. Others are graphics. One mailing was a map that pinpointed all of StreetGlow's distributors.

Experts in direct mailings stress the value of making such contacts as personal as possible because the company is talking directly to its customers. Such mailings are far more effective if sent to a specific name, rather than "occupant." Some marketers even recommend hand addressing the envelope if the message is about a special activity in which the company wants its customers to be involved. The message should always convey a benefit to the recipient. As Jack discovered, the message can be long, especially if sent to active customers, distributors, or others who have an interest in the product or company. Even the announcement about the newest product in StreetGlow's line is interesting to such an audience.

The most important factor is that the mailings are regular and consistent. Jack has never had a customer ask to be removed from his mailing list. In fact, he has received many compliments. Even better, he has received lots of sales. StreetGlow was on the *Inc.* magazine list of the 500 fastest-growing, privately owned companies in America three years in a row.

■　■　■

Tips for improving your marketing mailings to customers:

- Send your messages on a regular basis.

- Make the contents and address as personal as possible.

- Strive to make your mailing stand out in a stack of letters. Don't use standard white envelopes.

- Make the benefit clear and prominent.

- Encourage the customer to take some action and set a deadline.

- If you send postcards, keep the information concise. If you send a regular letter, provide answers to everything your customer is likely to want to know.

- Use first class postage stamps, not bulk mail and metered postage.

- Test different messages and other elements such as photos, graphics, or maps.

57.   BUILD YOUR OWN
MAILING LIST

Define your most-likely client and then carefully build and
maintain a contact list of people who fit your definition.

■ ■ ■

Bob Wietzke is both a certified public accountant in Ohio and North
Carolina and a certified valuation analyst, but when he started Valuation
Professionals Inc. in Southern California in 1989, the letters CPA and
CVA had little meaning to most business owners even though those owners often need to know the value of their companies for estate planning,
mergers and acquisitions, divestitures, and lawsuits. Bob decided to build
a mailing list of likely clients to whom he could mail marketing materials
and newsletters.

Direct mail marketing can be an attention grabber or trashcan fodder.
The key is getting a targeted list that reaches the right people. Once
you've been in business for a while, current and past customers should be
at the top of the mailing list. But when you're first starting, the challenge
is to identify the type of person most likely to need your products or services. Instead of appealing directly to the owners of companies, Bob
combed through the Martindale-Hubbell directory of attorneys for those
who specialized in estate planning. These trusted advisors are involved in
the legal situations that require a business valuation and are usually the
ones who recommend the appraiser to hire. "Now Martindale-Hubbell is
on the Internet (http://www.martindale.com), but back then I had to go to
the library. It took me hours to build my database; I had to screen each
entry." In addition to legal specialty, Bob studied each attorney's resume,
background, and age. He concluded that regional firms of one or two
attorneys were his target market. Why? "Large firms just wanted to deal
with big business valuation firms because they equate big with good,
which in my industry isn't true," Bob says. "In the beginning, I was a single consultant, and they thought, 'Who is this guy?' even though I had 22
years of experience in major accounting firms, public companies, and
investment banking."

Bob bought a professionally prepared, although generic, newsletter onto which Valuation Professionals was printed. "It's important that the mailing be of high quality," he explains. He started mailing the newsletter to the attorneys, later adding specialists in litigation and employee stock ownership plans and certified public accountants who worked in estate planning. "A few people asked to be removed from my mailing list, but not many," Bob says. "Those who did, I probably wouldn't want to do business with anyway."

The list grew to 800 names and built the foundation for Bob's client list, which ranges from candy manufacturers to a chain of coin-operated laundries. However, a printed newsletter is expensive, $3 or $4 each including postage, envelope, and an assistant's time to prepare the mailing, a major reason many companies have moved such publications to the Internet. Yet regular mail personally addressed stands out in a mailbox. Cost forced Bob to cull his list to the 500 best referral firms, clients, and prospects. Now he regularly adds to, trims, and updates the mailing list. He mails the newsletters first class so that he receives notice when a person moves. That fact, in addition to the tendency of people to open first-class letters more frequently than bulk mail, makes the extra postage cost worth the money. Even with a targeted list, the marketer must be patient, Bob says. "They don't necessarily call me right away. Sometimes they save every issue and years later call me when they need a valuation."

■ ■ ■

Tips for building an effectively targeted mailing list:

■ Start with current and past clients.

■ Include colleagues, friends, and other names known to match your most-likely client.

■ Add to your list over time as you receive referrals.

■ Develop on your Web site the means to capture names and contact information and add these visitors to your list.

■ Continually cull and update your mailing list. Eliminate names that no longer qualify. Note address, phone number, and e-mail changes.

58.   DIRECT MAIL
TO 100,000

If you buy a mailing list for marketing purposes,
it's vital that the people on the list match as
closely as possible your ideal clients.

■ ■ ■

Kerry Osaki was a newcomer to the law practice of Jeff Wheatley when the firm launched its first direct mail campaign in 1988. The practice, which started in the 1970s, specializes in construction law, so instead of buying a generic list of local businesses, they bought the list of licensed builders from the state contractors licensing board. Kerry and Jeff decided to buy only the 100,000 names in Southern California. The rule of thumb is that direct mail advertising gets a 1 percent response. However, some mailings do much worse; some much better. Having an attractive and timely offer is certainly important, but getting the mail piece to the right person at the right company is the key to success. The closer the people on a mailing list match the most-likely buyer for your product or service, the better the response. If you can't mail to current or former clients, you have to buy a mailing list. But a careful assessment beforehand about whom you want to reach will mean the difference between a successful direct mail campaign and a failure.

Kerry's law firm, now called Wheatley, Osaki, and Associates in Fullerton, California, couldn't handle the workload if all 100,000 contractors called in response to a mailing, Kerry says, so the firm mailed to approximately 30,000 names at a time, three times a year. Each mailing targeted a specific geographic region within Southern California. "Sometimes we included our newsletter in the mailing. Other times we sent just a postcard stating 'free legal advice' and the toll-free number of our construction law hot line," Kerry says.

Giving recipients multiple, easy ways to contact the company, such as toll-free telephone numbers and e-mail addresses, is important. However, the attorneys found that the word *free* is magic. "People call and say, 'I can't believe this. Free from an attorney?'" Kerry laughs. "I always explain that answering one question is not that big a deal, and then we hope to generate good will so when they need an attorney, they'll think of that nice attorney who answered their question."

It's a little difficult for Kerry to say precisely the response rate he gets from mailings. He has received calls from people who have kept a postcard for eight years before following up because they finally had a need for legal advice or work. Rising postal costs and the established client base—which brings repeat and referral business—have allowed Kerry to reduce the number of people to whom he mails. Still, each mailing goes to 20,000 people. He receives immediate calls from about 200 people. "We work constantly to clean up the list," Kerry says. "It costs too much to be mailing to addresses after the person has moved."

When Kerry joined the firm he had six clients. Now, thanks in large part to the continuing mailings, he has hundreds. Jeff has retired. "Our direct mail has kept us in business through two recessions," Kerry says.

■ ■ ■

Tips for improving your direct mail advertising:

- Buy a great mailing list that closely aligns with your target market.

- Don't use mailing labels. Use a laser printer or addressing machine to ink the address directly on the envelope.

- A call to action, such as "call us today for an appointment" increases response rate.

- Use the word *you* as often as possible in the direct mail piece. Use the word *I* almost never.

- Don't put too much information on the envelope. It screams "junk."

- Test the letter or advertising piece to a few hundred names before mailing to millions, and change the offer (i.e., one version says two for the price of one; the other says 50 percent off) to see which one gets a better response.

- Make sure your staff knows about the promotional mailing so they give a knowledgeable, friendly response.

59. COMMUNICATION THAT SERVES DOUBLE DUTY

Every contact with your customers can double
as a marketing opportunity.

■ ■ ■

When a potential customer asks Carolyn Minerich to fax a price quote for a project, she might also send a flier about the 24-foot metal tree recently made by her company, Carmin Industries in Jacksonville, Alabama. If someone requests a brochure, Carolyn might enclose in the envelope a separate sheet about the company's waterjet cutting capabilities.

Unsolicited faxes, telemarketing phone calls, and e-mails have generated so much public anger that Congress and some state legislatures have outlawed them. So when someone actually invites you to communicate with them—whether by mail, telephone, fax, or e-mail—make that contact do double duty in marketing your company's products and services. Major corporations, from credit card companies to utilities, have used this double-duty mailing for years. Some even use it as a moneymaker, enclosing information about unrelated products for a fee. But such marketing may be counterproductive. Too many inserts about too many different subjects can annoy customers and dilute your own marketing message.

That message can inform or educate your customers about capabilities they don't even know you offer. Carmin Industries can do welding, painting, and precision machining, all of which are common. But few people understand precision waterjet cutting, which is Carmin Industries' specialty. "They say, 'the last thing I need is a boat,'" Carolyn says. "I have to tell them about the huge figures we have cut for Disney World. You'll find our components on the Islands of Adventure at Universal Studios in Florida, at the Hawaii Convention Center, and in the U.S. Air Force." The waterjet method can precision cut aluminum as thin as 0.125 of an inch or as thick as six inches. It can cut glass, ceramic, and stone, and it can cut intricate shapes from numerals to 24-foot trees. So Carolyn started enclosing fliers about Carmin waterjet cutting projects in the company's regular mailings and invoices in 1998. Later she added the flier as a second page to faxed price quotes requested by customers for other work.

"I'm gun-shy about mass faxes because of laws, but no one complains about an extra page on faxes they have asked for," she says. "The fax campaign is the best I ever did." No one has ever objected to receiving an extra sheet of paper, which they might if Carolyn sent it separately and unsolicited. In fact, many of the recipients appreciate the information. "You never know where that sheet will end up," she says. "I've gotten calls from architects who said, 'I've had your flier in my drawer for six months. Now I've got a special design, and I want to know if Carmin can make it.'"

■　■　■

Ways to multiply the effects of customer communications:

- Selling promotion space in mailed monthly billings

- Listing other capabilities, services, and products with faxed pricing quotes

- Reminding customers of your company's core competencies in a tagline of e-mail reply for information

- Recommending complementary products in mailed invoices for services

- Suggesting additional, complementary items when customers are placing orders for your main product

- Attaching a business card to thank you notes or birthday cards mailed to customers

- Attaching a flier offering a discount to your product's packaging

- Listing current offers sent with auto-responder e-mails to people who request information

60.   NEWSLETTERS THAT SELL

A great-looking newsletter is an unsuccessful marketing tool if it doesn't boost your business.

■ ■ ■

Ron Loutherback had owned restaurants and a tavern before, but he wanted to turn his interest in fine wine into a successful wine shop. First he opened a delicatessen that sold wine in 1975. Then, listening to the desires of customers, he opened The Wine Club in Santa Ana, California, in 1985 as a low-markup warehouse shop with reasonably priced samples and knowledgeable sales staff. Still the business struggled, making a profit in only four months during the first three years it was open.

In February 1988, Ron attended a seminar on how to produce newsletters that sell. "I'd had a newsletter since 1975 but it wasn't selling wine," he says. "It's not for entertainment; it's there to sell something." What Ron learned in the seminar was that a selling newsletter needs a headline, story, and sale closer. The cover should pull readers inside, the way a good headline encourages them to read a story. The stories and wine reviews must be interesting, and the reviews must close the sale. "Most of our reviews are written in-house," Ron says. "Some writers think the price sells the wine. That's baloney. How about something basic like 'Wouldn't you like to take a bottle home with you today?'"

The articles can still be interesting and the artwork attractive, but they must not block the marketing purpose of the newsletter or it's a waste of money, in Ron's view. Over the years, Ron gently battled with his newsletter editors and graphic artists about how to achieve a newsletter that sells.

Ron started advertising in regional publications the fact that customers didn't have to drive to the shop to buy wine, but instead could call for a newsletter and order by mail. "We stressed convenience—just pick up the phone. You don't have to drive for miles. You don't have to fill out a form," Ron says.

Thousands of people responded.

"Wine nuts want to read about wines. The articles are mostly reviews of wines," Ron says. That helps reenforce the belief in customers' minds that The Wine Club staff really knows the merchandise. The Wine Club's mailing list grew from 2,000 names to 8,000 very quickly just by promoting it in print advertising. "I started offering a free cork puller, which cost me $13, to customers who gave us the name and address of four of their wine-loving friends," Ron says. "Our mailing list went to 97,000. And the newsletter was the primary reason for our big growth in the '90s."

Marjorie Loutherback had to make 3,000 changes a month to keep the mailing list current, an important factor in successful newsletters that sell. Within months, The Wine Club was profitable and has enjoyed double-digit annual growth for years. The company opened stores in San Francisco and Santa Clara, California. Ron credits the newsletter for playing an important role in making The Wine Club the largest wine store west of the Mississippi. Some customers spend more than a million dollars a year at The Wine Club. "The newsletter is our number one sales tool today," Ron says. The company Web site is a companion sales tool and offers free subscriptions to the newsletter as well. The newsletter grew substantially over the years to 36 pages with a color cover photograph. Many of the pages list specific wines by brand, year, score, Wine Club price, and which of the three stores carries it. One of the toughest jobs for the newsletter editor is reconciling available inventory and location. Most bottles are sold in less than 30 days, and exceptional wines, like 2000 vintage Bordeaux, are presold before they ever hit the market.

■　■　■

How to create a newsletter that sells:

- Determine whether your type of business and clientele will benefit from a newsletter. Your mailing list should be at least 500 names.

- Decide if sales will justify the postage and printing costs of a regular newsletter or if your clientele will be just as receptive to an e-mailed newsletter.

- Create a distinctive look. It shouldn't look like an ad.

- Develop quality content that matches your clientele's interests.

- Commit time to the newsletter. It must be published consistently over a long period of time to affect sales.

- Always include some call to action and track the response so you can properly evaluate the effectiveness of the newsletter.

61. PUBLISH A CATALOG

The expense of a catalog can be justified only
if you plan to build a substantial company.

■ ■ ■

Lisa Hammond was managing a construction company in 1996 when she thought a catalog business would be a creative outlet, a vehicle to inspire and help other women . . . and fun. A year later she mailed the first catalog for Femail Creations in Las Vegas, Nevada. Femail Creations was to be a company by, for, and about women. Its artwork, clothing, and other products were from women artists and women-owned companies. Lisa had no experience with catalogs, other than shopping from them because she liked the time savings and convenience of shopping when she could and having products delivered right to her door.

Catalogs started in the 1800s when many Americans lived in rural areas far from any stores. These books are the backbone of the $2 trillion mail order industry, because today's American is busy and, like Lisa, loves convenience, wide selection, and quality products at prices often lower than retail. Lisa started Femail Creations with the products of 50 vendors, filling the catalog's pages with items from around her own home or that were meaningful to her. She worked 100-hour weeks and mortgaged her home to help finance the business.

"I did not expect starting a catalog to cost so much," she says. "It's a challenge to bootstrap it. You think it's going to be fun, but at the end of the day, there's no room in this industry for small businesses." Lisa initially thought Femail Creations could be a financial success with $1 million in sales annually. Now, she says a catalog company requires at least $3 million in investment and $15 million in revenues. The cost "has meant that profitability is a long time coming," Lisa says. "Unlike most businesses where three years is a benchmark to break even, it is more like seven to ten years for catalogs."

Femail Creations now works with 500 artists and more than 200 vendors. The inventory is an eclectic blend of paintings and other decor items; children's costumes and clothing; women's T-shirts, aprons, and other apparel; and jewelry and other accessories.

Many small retailers and manufacturers create their own catalogs as a supplement to their core sales. Some companies have simple, two-color leaflets with sketches instead of photographs, choose a size that fits a standard envelope, and mail to a restricted list of qualified customers. However, for businesses that rely on catalogs for most of their sales, the catalog must reflect the image and quality the company wants to convey, just as a store would. Its full-color photographs must show the products in enticing ways to lure buyers.

Femail Creations added a Web site because customers asked for one, although mail order still accounts for 65 percent of sales. "The perception is that it's cheaper [to run a mail-order business] online, but it's not," Lisa says. "The reality is that most of our online customers still want to have that catalog in hand and then order over the Internet.

■   ■   ■

Keys to a successful catalog:

- A well-researched financial plan so every cost is covered and each product makes money

- Enticing products

- A properly targeted and qualified market

- A competitive offer—it doesn't have to have lowest price, but does need to be the best value

- Persuasive design, copy, and photographs or illustrations

- Easy-to-follow ordering instructions

- A compelling call to buy immediately

- Continual freshening of the inventory

62. TOLL-FREE TELEPHONE NUMBER

More customers will call if you pick up the phone tab.

■ ■ ■

To make the dream of living in rural Maine a practical reality, Wendy and Jack Newmeyer had to find some way to pay the bills. Jack sold wood pulp from the trees on their 111 acres to nearby paper mills. Wendy grew and sold 120 varieties of herbs to restaurants and farmers' markets. Then in the early 1980s, she read a book that described balsam fir as an herb. Balsam is a fast growing tree that self-seeds very well and grows throughout the region near West Paris, Maine, where the Newmeyers live. So Wendy added balsam to her herb inventory. She was selling it for seven cents a pound. Then a Vermont woman offered to pay $1.75 a pound for ground-up balsam fir to be sewn into pillows sold mostly through souvenir shops. Wendy sat down and calculated that she personally could make 10,000 pillows annually of better quality than those currently on the market. So in 1984, she started shredding balsam fir and created Maine Balsam Fir Products Inc. selling pillows to gift shops.

Almost immediately, she was getting national interest in her pillows.

"I knew how I was. If there were two companies with something I wanted and one had a toll-free number, I would call the 800 number," Wendy says. So she invested in a toll-free number as well. She picked 1-800-5BALSAM, but has not advertised the number that way because so many people hate to figure out the numbers corresponding to those letters. The toll-free number was an instant hit with gift shop owners. "We used to get orders in the mail," Wendy recalls. "After we got the 800 number, [the mail orders] stopped over night."

Maine Balsam has 5,000 retailers on its customer list, 500 of which are core customers and another 1,000 of which order less often but still regularly. The company buys 100,000 pounds of balsam, mostly from other small farms in the area, and sells 100,000 pillows, draft stoppers, trivets, and other items each year. Maine Balsam's monthly bill for toll-free service has averaged $250 over the years. The company's wholesale orders average $300. If just one more person is encouraged to place an order because of the free phone call, it pays the entire month's bill, Wendy says. Maine Balsam also gets a few retail orders by phone, usually in the fall.

Balsam has a subtle, long-lasting fragrance that reminds people of Christmas and summer vacations spent in the woods. Balsam pillows become family heirlooms. "People have a real affection for this product. It's almost beyond logic," Wendy says. "They have childhood memories of New England." If they put an ad in *Yankee* or *Down East* magazines, a thousand people call. The company mails out a catalog and has a Web site. "We get more inquiries from the Internet, but people still want to call to place an order," Wendy says.

■ ■ ■

Tips for making a toll-free telephone number work for your business:

- Analyze how your business will use the number before investing.

- Calculate costs and estimate potential increased income to make sure you can afford the line.

- Charges and services vary by telephone company, so shop around and look for hidden costs.

- Promote the toll-free number on all marketing materials and company stationery.

- Realize that two-thirds of calls to toll-free numbers are not for orders and plan a strategy to maximize the benefit of those calls.

- Prepare in case the toll-free line substantially increases your workload.

- Many phone bills identify where calls come from and when they come in. Use that information in your marketing plans.

63. FREELY ILLUSTRATE YOUR EXPERTISE

Giving potential customers an example of your work can be a
more cost-effective marketing tool than paid advertisements.

■ ■ ■

When John DeLasaux launched InLynx as a computer-networking
expert in Phoenix, Arizona, in 1998, he discovered that potential clients
love something for nothing. His most effective means to build InLynx's
client base was to give a free network evaluation and written report on the
condition of the potential client's computer network and the work that
would be required to bring it up to standard. "This was a lot of extra work
for the engineers, but it had a very high closing rate—95 percent—because
the engineers had the opportunity to talk to the prospect and demonstrate
their networking skills right on the prospect's system," John says.

Service providers always walk a tightrope in demonstrating enough
skill and expertise to win a contract without giving away everything that
they're in business to sell. The key is to provide the tasty tidbit without
handing over the whole cookie jar. InLynx strives to develop long-term
strategic relationships with clients in order to gain their computer networking business for Microsoft Windows and Novell products. The written report usually leads to designing, deploying, and managing IT systems.

The written report works well, John says, because it can easily be
turned into a written scope of work that results in the contracts that his clients sign and which clearly document the timing and price of each phase
of work. "The extra work of writing it all down was well worth it because
it was a project scheduling and control document, a baseline for change
control purposes, [and] gave a yardstick which the client could easily use
to get a clear picture about how good our service was," John says. "It
reduced the number of disagreements with clients about what was done
and whether it was done as agreed." That approach meant that InLynx met
client expectations. "As a result, we had no problem eliciting letters of
referral from most of our clients," he says. "We are not bashful at all about
asking our clients for referrals, because they appreciate our service and

want their friends to benefit from the same kind of treatment that they get from us."

However, the free reports had a downside, John says. They were costly to prepare and very tiring for the engineers who spent countless hours generating so much written documentation. "The only relief comes when another prospect accepts your report and signs on the dotted line," he says. "As a strategy for building business, it was a necessity. As a continuing mode of operation, it causes burnout of the key employees."

Therefore, after InLynx developed a track record and strong enough client base, it cut back on the free written reports. "We use the free evaluation only in cases where we really want to target a certain prospect [that we are] sure we can't close any other way," John says.

■ ■ ■

Tips for enticing customers with tidbits without undermining the sale:

■ Keep your giveaways to samples. Don't give away the full report.

■ Show enough to demonstrate value without exposing the proprietary information and company expertise that is your bread and butter.

■ Develop a simple list of questions to help you screen good prospects from those who only want something for nothing.

■ Write pamphlets of commonly asked questions and answers or give abbreviated workshops.

■ Clarify in your own mind the dividing line between the free sample and the giveaway that's the core of your business.

■ Avoid overextending your employees in providing the free information.

■ Once you've given away your standard free advice, tell questioners that additional time and information will be charged at your usual hourly rate.

64.   COLD CALLS

Cold calling must have a targeted message
for a targeted audience to be effective.

■ ■ ■

Dick Engel is both a staffing consultant and headhunter for scientists, engineers, and information technology specialists. When he wants to find a scientist with security clearance for federal defense projects, he picks up the telephone. When he wants to find consulting clients for his company, Pragmatic Systems & Staffing LLC in Scottsdale, Arizona, he picks up the telephone. Not because it's easy but because it works. "When I owned another business in the 1980s, I looked at the telephone knowing that I had to make calls, and I thought of it as a two-headed monster," Dick says. Then he spent a while in the early 1990s working for Robert Half International, an international staffing company, he was trained at cold calling and measured on the number of calls made. That training has proven effective for Pragmatic Systems.

In spite of the National Do Not Call Registry for telemarketers and the marketing firms pushing Internet selling techniques, the telephone is still a valuable marketing tool when used in connection with other marketing techniques and strategies. A single call, like an isolated advertisement, doesn't work. Yet cold calling doesn't mean random telephone dialing and trying to elicit work from whoever answers. The people you call should be the people who want to buy and can afford what you're selling—the higher up the company decision-making ladder the better, Dick says. "Getting the correct name is often an art form, unless you are lucky enough to find or buy a list with the target people," he says. "I want to find the most influential person in making the hiring decision."

Dick works with two types of clients: those who have the jobs, such as government agencies, and those with the special skills in unusual fields. He works on behalf of a lot of small or mid-sized companies. Federal law requires its major agencies to try to give some contracts to small business. So Dick might find out the name of the contract administrator for a specific project at a federal defense contractor. When he calls that person he doesn't say, "If you need people, call me." He says, "Are you meeting your small business quota?"

Pragmatic Systems specializes in finding workers for projects that require security clearance. Dick finds many of his initial contact names at niche job Web sites, but it's rarely a perfect match for the job he's trying to fill. "These are needle-in-a-haystack searches," Dick says. "I might still call the names I get and ask who they know who matches what I'm looking for. Then it becomes a warm referral to the name they give me." Such calling works if you're persistent and constant in your efforts, Dick says. He sets a daily goal of 15 telephone calls to a targeted audience with his targeted message or search. "That's not just dialing 15 phone numbers. It's making 15 good, qualified connections," he says. "Voice mail and no answer don't count."

As the owner of a small firm, Dick is responsible for many different management, financial, and marketing tasks, so it is tempting not to put in the time and effort necessary to make cold calling work. Even though Dick has telephone training and repeated success with cold calling, "it is still my least favorite activity. It does not come naturally; it takes a lot of work."

■　■　■

Tips for cold calling:

- Don't call randomly. You still need a good list of qualified potential customers.

- Use phone calls in connection with other forms of marketing, not by itself.

- Prepare to commit time and effort to telephone calls.

- Don't use trickery and deception when trying to reach an executive by telephone.

- Your telephone techniques will improve with practice and training.

- If you don't prepare a script, at least spend time clarifying the major points you will want to touch on during the telephone conversation.

- Quit making excuses. Set daily goals for more effective cold calling.

PART 8

EXPOSURE

■ ■ ■

You don't have to be a striptease artist to expose yourself and your business to a broad audience. But you do have to learn how to perform. Your performance will differ, depending on the medium you choose. Despite the rise of 500 cable television channels and the steady decline in the number of newspapers, print is still the most common medium for exposure that serves a marketing purpose. Print includes daily and weekly newspapers, trade and consumer magazines, newsletters, and even books. Many business owners who are competent writers can have a powerful marketing impact by writing articles and columns themselves. However, being included in an article written by a disinterested third party carries an impact that writing about yourself doesn't.

The most important point of media exposure is to learn how to perform—that is, to craft a short and simple message that resonates with the audience. Just as your customer views your products or services through the personal filter of What's in it for me? so does the newspaper reader, television viewer, or radio listener. It is definitely uppermost in the mind of the customer looking through the telephone directory for a company to solve some specific need. Believe it or not, it's the unspoken question of audience members at public speeches or seminars. With that in mind, develop your message as the best answer available to that question.

65. ATTRACT ATTENTION WITH PUBLIC RELATIONS

Media coverage gives your company a valuable
third-party endorsement that money can't buy.

■ ■ ■

Debra Cohen gave up a high-salaried corporate job in Manhattan to stay at home with her infant daughter in Hewlett on Long Island in New York. Still, she wanted a home-based business. She found the right business, literally, in her 75-year-old Tudor home that needed professional home-improvement work. Debra created Home Remedies of NY Inc. to link homeowners with prescreened, reliable home contractors. She contacted the local newspaper about her business and when the editor said, "Send me something," Debra thought, "Uh oh." With the help of a friend in public relations, Debra put together a pitch letter and related information, and the resulting story caused her business to explode.

Media coverage, she learned, works like a third-party endorsement about a business. "Once I realized the impact that press attention could have on my business, I created a press kit and continually pitched different story ideas to publications that reach my target audience," Debra says.

News and feature stories about Home Remedies also opened a second revenue stream. Other would-be home-business entrepreneurs contacted Debra to learn how she set up her company. She wrote *The Complete Guide to Owning and Operating a Successful Homeowner Referral Network* and started selling Homeowner Referral Network (HRN) business opportunities. She has sold more than 350 of the HRN business opportunities worldwide.

"I would say that my expansion and success are a direct result of a good PR campaign," she says.

Debra is always thinking about stories related to home repair that she can pitch to appropriate media. It is important to contact the right editor or reporter and to have a story they can use. But there's a fine line between being a good media resource and a pest. She has learned not to be too aggressive in seeking stories because many editors and reporters don't like to write about something the competition recently covered. The coverage and the type of businesses she runs have put Debra on the experts' list for some reporters. *Smart Money* magazine has interviewed her about wise choices in home improvement projects. CNN cable television and *Entrepreneur* magazine ran stories about her business. She writes an online advice column on home-based businesses. Most coverage gives a tremendous, immediate boost to her business and to her HRN customer businesses.

"But you can't always tell. Sometimes, I get little reaction, but when the Lifetime Television show *New Attitudes* and *Parents* magazine did stories, I got tremendous business," Debra says. The readership of a publication or audience of a television show makes a difference, she adds. Her biggest boost seems to come when the audience includes parents who want to work from home. In addition to the initial business boost from an article, Debra derives continuing benefit from the coverage by sending reprints of the articles in her direct mail campaigns. In such cases, the business owner may need to pay a fee to avoid copyright infringement.

■ ■ ■

Tips for working with the media:

- Ask yourself how the reader or viewer will benefit from your story and craft your pitch accordingly.

- Understand what news is: rarity, proximity, prominence, about people, crises, timeliness, and impact. Stress those aspects of your story, if possible.

- Target the medium whose audiences are most likely to be interested in your story.

- Find out the name and title of the specific editor or reporter to contact.

- Be mindful of publications' deadlines for specific sections or features.

- Don't expect to be notified if your story runs. If you absolutely must know, hire a clipping service.

- Be honest. Don't make claims you can't prove.

- Be an expert. Develop your ability to cite statistics and facts about your subject.

- Don't tell reporters anything you don't want to see in print.

- Understand that your story won't always be used. Each time it is used, analyze what made that idea or story angle appealing.

66. THE DOWNSIDE OF PRESS COVERAGE

You don't control stories you don't pay for and you
have little recourse if stories are unfair.

■ ■ ■

Mary and Rick Jurmain wanted to give teenagers a realistic experience of the responsibilities of parenthood when they created an infant simulator called Baby Think It Over in 1993. The company, which is now called Realityworks Inc. in Eau Claire, Wisconsin, really started to take off after *USA Today* ran an article about the product. The public was concerned about the high rate of teen pregnancies at the time, but Baby Think It Over had a broader educational purpose of teaching parenting responsibilities, car seat safety, and careful treatment such as not shaking an infant. Other newspapers, television stations, and magazines, including *People* and the *New York Times,* picked up the story and the publicity jump-started orders.

Such free publicity is usually a boon to a fledgling company with little or no advertising budget. But it can have a downside, Mary says. "Although most of our media attention was favorable, occasionally we were unpleasantly surprised by inaccurate or unfair stories."

One newspaper editor ran a very negative and inaccurate editorial about Baby Think It Over. "In the early years, I was passionate about our product, and I wrote a letter to the editor that I was outraged by the unfairness," Mary recalls. Her letter ran, and then the editor wrote an even more scathing editorial and didn't publish Mary's second letter in defense of her product. "That's when I learned you can't fight the press like that; he's in control" of what is published.

Another time, a reporter from a major U.S. newspaper, although friendly during a telephone interview, wrote that Baby Think It Over was a useless product and cited one study that had not followed the company's instructions for using the product. "The story made it sound like this was the only study out there, but there were seven or eight others that showed positive impact," Mary says. "What was worse, they ran a photo of our most recent product so it was as if the study had been done on that product, which it hadn't."

Even if a publication runs a correction, relatively few people see it, she says. "Honest errors I don't mind, but what I object to are reporters who come to a story with an ax to grind." It's a mistake to stop talking to reporters, she adds. "You shoot yourself in the foot, and if you talk to them, you at least stand a chance of getting your side told."

Mary learned to be proactive in interviews and not wait for reporters to ask the right questions to get her point across. She stresses, without being asked, that Baby Think It Over isn't just about preventing teen pregnancies but to giving participants a realistic experience of infant care and child safety. Mary also groomed her assistant to take over the position of full-time public relations and community affairs manager. That gives Mary more time to oversee Realityworks' expansion into other realistic learning products such as NICoteen, which demonstrates the consequences of smoking; The Gamble, which explores the effects of drug and alcohol use on unborn babies; and The Juggling Act, an interactive financial education and time-management program.

■ ■ ■

Tips for preparing for an interview:

- Clarify your own message. It helps to write a motto to succinctly state what business you're really in.

- If you pitched a story idea to a publication, review it before the interview.

- Develop a list of talking points that you want to get across, even if the reporter doesn't ask.

■ If the reporter requests the interview, ask what the point of the story is.

■ Have a company background story, brief resume, and photo available to give the reporter or editor.

■ Read the publication, view the television show, or listen to the radio program before the interview, if possible.

■ Practice being interviewed.

67. CAPITALIZE ON CLIENT RESEARCH

Use know-how developed while serving clients to establish
your credentials as an expert source with the media.

■ ■ ■

Several times a week, John Challenger sends data, survey results, or analysis of government reports to a huge list of media representatives. Thousands of them—from CBS television news to Agence France Presse in Paris—have used his material. Sometimes the information is campy, such as Halloween hiring trends, and other times it is serious, like the number of Americans who have been out of work for 27 weeks. It's all information that John needs to know as chief executive of Challenger, Gray & Christmas Inc., a Chicago, Illinois–based company that helps laid-off workers and executives find other jobs.

"My father, who started the company in the mid-1960s, started doing the surveys in the early 1980s for our customers," John says. "About the mid- to late 1980s we started sharing them with the press. It's a great way of converting information we get from our business."

John's clients are companies making staff cutbacks. "The reports are a way of showing them that they've done well by those people, helping them transition to another job," John says. "We started doing statistics, such as the length of time it takes people to find a new job at equal or better pay." That kind of information is of interest to the public as well. As newspapers and magazines have increased their business coverage, their need for experts about the job market has increased as well. Trade journals, human resources publications, and television talk shows also need experts. The reports and surveys have helped establish John, as spokesman for Challenger, Gray & Christmas, as such an expert.

The company's expansion to national and, more recently, international markets has enhanced John's research. He can gather a great deal of information by tracking his own clients and their former employees' job searches. Over the years he has surveyed how many executives start new businesses rather than take another job, how long it takes executives to find work, and whether they make more money. But he supplements his own research with government reports, such as the number of jobless claims or the number of temporary jobs that retailers add at Christmas. He also makes note of major companies' activities that could affect the job market. If IBM announces it will create 10,000 jobs this year, John sticks that information in his file. If Hyundai invests money in a new U.S. plant, he adds that to the mix. Then occasionally, John will group these actions together in a press release and comment on the apparent job trend. "We're always thinking about these things, so we started writing about them," John explains. "It's a great marketing tool. Certainly it is a piece of our success. Not all our growth is attributable to these surveys and press coverage of them. We also had to build a good, strong sales force." But that sales force always has plenty of fresh press clippings of articles that quote John as evidence that Challenger, Gray & Christmas knows the job market better than anyone.

■ ■ ■

Samples of information to collect:

■ Keep statistics on your industry in the marketplace; i.e., a real estate broker tracking home sales.

■ Survey your customers and suppliers about industry trends.

■ Set up a periodic poll of members of your trade association and track responses over time.

- Compile and analyze data that are publicly available such as census, Internal Revenue Service, and other government data. (Government documents aren't copyrighted.)

- Summarize industry-specific information from research done by universities and trade groups.

68. LAUNCH YOUR OWN PUBLICATION

Publishing your own magazine or newspaper can
gain exposure and build business faster than relying
on coverage in third-party publications.

■ ■ ■

Jacqueline Andrews has started three different networking groups in Hawaii and California over a 20-year period. Each time, she has also developed a tabloid-sized newspaper to gain exposure for the group and its members. "It's a perfect vehicle," Jacqueline explains. "Members advertise. New members are attracted because of the journal, and members get business for each other." Her current referral exchange organization in Laguna Niguel, California, is called Integrity Pros, and the publication is *Integrity Business and Consumer Journal.* After the corporate scandals of the early 2000s, both entrepreneurs and consumers are looking for people of integrity with which to do business, Jacqueline says. She personally checks out each new member business, meeting the owner in person, visiting the business facilities, and checking the products and services. "If I get complaints, I take them off the list," Jacqueline says.

Jacqueline first started the journal as a way to promote her referral organization and its members, but each time, the publication became a money-making success in its own right. Members can buy advertisements in the Integrity Journal, paying from $190 per quarter for a small ad up to $1,550 for a full page. The articles are upbeat and encouraging, such as "Why Should I Network" and "Characteristics of an Optimist." The Journal is laced with quotes such as "Falling down doesn't make you a failure but staying down does." Members of Integrity Pros also submit articles and artwork.

"The more the journal is out there, the easier it is to get content," Jacqueline says. Content is important to get people to read the publication, seek out the referral group, and give business to the advertising members. "It's upbeat so people read it," she says. "I never realized that the market for personal and business encouragement was so rare and in such demand."

Jacqueline didn't own a computer or even know how to type when she put out her first promotional publication in the 1980s. Computers now make the process easier. She can e-mail the journal to some people, but she also publishes the 12-page journal on newsprint. The newspaper-like format costs more but attracts more advertising than an electronic newsletter would, she says.

She distributes the printed version all over Southern California. "I get permission, and put it in libraries, Office Depot locations, restaurants, coffee shops, and car washes," she says. "About half the places I ask say yes." That additional circulation is important for growing the Integrity Pros referral group and for benefiting members who write articles and advertise. The more widely Jacqueline can distribute the *Integrity Journal,* the more effective a marketing tool it becomes. However, the *Integrity Journal* is a hands-on, high-labor form of marketing. "It does require skills different from leading a referral group for successful people," Jacqueline says. "It's not easy. I work at it." But three times, the referral group-marketing publication has been a winning combination and business.

■　■　■

Tips to creating your own successful publication:

- Determine the theme related to your expertise and industry.

- Develop sources of good stories and other content. A publication full of puff pieces and self-promotion will just be thrown away.

- Figure out a means to distribute the publication to your target audience.

- Seek advertising and other revenue streams to offset publication costs.

- Encourage complementary businesses to participate in the publication, but retain editorial control yourself.

- Find ways to work the publication into other areas of your business so that they promote each other.

69. THE WRITE WAY
TO ESTABLISH YOUR AUTHORITY

Published articles and books can substantiate your expertise
and credentials with a widespread and varied audience.

■ ■ ■

Michael LeBoeuf was a management professor teaching time management at the University of New Orleans when a friend suggested that he turn his class notes into a book while on sabbatical. "I was becoming disenchanted with the academic life," Michael says. "I figured I didn't want to teach until I was 65." His plan was to publish books that would validate his reputation as a business expert leading to an independent career giving paid speeches to corporations and seminars on business topics he knew well, including productivity, creativity, and customer service. "A book is a credential," Michael says. "People who read the books and listen to the audio versions hire me to speak. What better way to market yourself than a book?"

Michael's plan received a boost when a change in the university's pension allowed him to retire early. "It was never my goal to build a company or be on the road 200 days a year," he says. "I wanted to be financially independent." The books indeed opened doors for dozens of speaking and consulting assignments each year. He worked with such giants as IBM, Xerox, and Shell Oil. But he also accepted projects with banks and medical practices. As a significant aspect of Michael's plan of independent self-employment, the books became a substantial profit center in themselves. The first book, *Working Smart,* sold more than 300,000 copies. *The Perfect Business* describes starting a one-person business just as he did. *How to Win Customers and Keep Them for Life* was his best seller. "I wrote about what interested me," Michael says. "The customer service book was very successful. The least successful was the book about productivity. People don't what to read about that."

While hundreds of thousands of nonfiction books are written each year, relatively few are picked up by publishing houses. That is why many people who want a book for marketing purposes pay to publish the work themselves. They distribute these books like calling cards or press kits to potential clients, companies, and the media. Other writers use their skills to market themselves through articles in journals, Web sites and other publications in their field of expertise or the market they want to target. They receive a biographical credit line with each article.

Michael's writing skill and choice of saleable topics appealed to many book publishers. He has worked with about half a dozen over the years. With his first book, Michael followed a friend's advice to write two sample chapters and a proposal stating the book's subject matter, why it was different from other self-help time management books, and what it would sell. He visited a local bookstore and made a list of 36 publishers who might be interested in such a book, then started mailing out the proposals. After the first book was published, getting other publishers and an agent was easier. "It's not a very creative plan," Michael says, "but it works."

■ ■ ■

Outlets where your writing skills can be used as a marketing tool:

- Books—the choice of publisher depends on your target market

- Articles or opinion pieces for newspapers and magazines whose readership is the market you are trying to reach

- Letters to the editor

- Syndicated columns

- Articles for content Web sites and e-zines

- Tips, informational items, and articles for your own Web site—distribute them free to other Web sites for broader exposure

- In-depth reports for trade groups, independent think tanks, and advocacy groups for your target market

70. ENABLE OTHERS TO ESTABLISH YOUR CREDIBILITY

While your own marketing can gain exposure for your company, others using your products can produce results that are even more credible and have broader reach.

■ ■ ■

Echelon Biosciences in Salt Lake City, Utah, has been extraordinarily successful for a research and development biotechnology company. Most such companies bleed buckets of red ink. They are laughingly referred to as "pharmaceutical companies unencumbered by revenues." But Echelon Biosciences made money from its inception in 1997, even though it has no outside investors. Its annual sales now exceed $1 million and are growing 40 percent a year. In fact, those sales contribute to Echelon's marketing strategy, says President W. Tim Miller.

Echelon was founded by Glenn Prestwich and C. Dale Poulter, chemistry professors at the University of Utah, and G. Thomas Heath, a graduate of the University of Utah. The mission of the venture was to discover and develop therapeutic compounds for the treatment of cancer, diabetes, and numerous infectious diseases. The company has developed biological compounds called reagents that are vital in research. Echelon does not only use these reagents in its own research. It sells these reagents and assays, which are analyses of materials that determine the nature of the ingredients, to other researchers worldwide. The customer list includes 300 pharmaceutical companies and universities in 30 countries. These transactions cost Echelon nothing except an occasional sample or a discounted price to a scientific collaborator who publishes the results involving the use of Echelon products. The collaborating researchers, in turn, publish the results of their use of Echelon reagents and assays in scientific journals. "It is the use of the scientific publications as our primary marketing tool that makes us unique," Tim explains. "In the scientific community, this is one of the key and credible means by which scientific progress is trumpeted. It builds awareness of the use and utility of our research reagents and assays. It promotes new uses. This leads to more publications and more sales."

Echelon's Web site lists more than 120 publications that cite the use of its products in research. The authors are leaders in their field so their research is credible and they enjoy large followings in the scientific community, Tim says. Their reputations further enhance Echelon's credibility and reputation. "This approach has worked from the beginning and has been one of the key drivers to product sales success," Tim says. "This has lead to a unique biotech model where we are not dependent on outside sources of capital for growth."

The sale of its reagents and assays fund Echelon's own research and development, which also has attracted research grants to work on discovering therapeutics for ovarian cancer and tuberculosis.

■ ■ ■

Determine if you have a marketing tool to sell:

■ Do you only think of the potential revenue sources within your business in terms of the finished products or services you make?

■ Have you created your own processes or tools that you use to make the products or develop services?

■ Can the process or device be adapted for others to use even in unrelated businesses?

■ Are you willing to let others be collaborators?

■ Can you structure the sale of your processes or tools to encourage repeat purchases?

■ How can you encourage the customers for this secondary part of your business to give you credit, thereby marketing your company at no cost to you?

71. ADVANCE NOTICE

To create interest and excitement, share your vision
as you build a new part of your business.

■ ■ ■

After owning a custom framing shop in northwest Mississippi, Loretta Lucius took the plunge and fulfilled her lifelong dream of making a living with her photography. She opened Lucius Studio in 1995, and soon had a steady business photographing weddings. That's when Loretta and her husband Joe decided to build a log wedding chapel on their property in Senatobia, Mississippi, to complement the successful wedding photography business. "We began marketing our wedding chapel the day after we decided to build it," Loretta says. "I wanted to get the word out that we were building a wedding chapel, not that we were thinking about building one."

Many entrepreneurs try to keep their new products or services under wraps until they're ready for market, but there is marketing value in creating excitement and interest in a product under development. Movies do it with trailers in the theaters as much as a year ahead of actual release. Automakers often display their concept cars years before they hit the market. This peek into the future can be an effective marketing tool for other entrepreneurs as well.

The Luciuses went to their first bridal show with blueprints in hand. Along with displays of wedding albums and portraits, the pair showed the floor plan of the chapel to be. Loretta immediately added the chapel plans to the company brochures and Web site with a "coming soon" caption. They researched existing wedding chapels, their distance from the Lucius property, and their layout. While shooting weddings, they counted the number of people to learn average attendance at such events and to know how large to build their Chapel in the Pines.

"We stirred up enough interest that potential customers watched the logs go up and toured the building before it had a roof," Loretta says. "I remember showing the alter area and bride's room by the blue chalk lines on the subfloor. One of our selling points was that we are four hours closer for Mississippi brides than the mountain chapels of east Tennessee."

Both Loretta and Joe carried business cards to give to potential future customers at weddings they photographed. Loretta made a point of chatting with young, single people and was keenly aware that many of them were watching the Luciuses work, dreaming ahead to their own weddings. Loretta set a goal of scheduling four weddings before the chapel opened. She got six. That also put pressure on the construction schedule, but everything was finished on time. The Chapel in the Pines opened in 2001. It has overtaken Loretta's photography business, hosting as many as three weddings a week. Loretta still does the wedding photography, but she also handles the paperwork, meets with prospective brides, and even learned to bake professional wedding cakes. Joe is an ordained minister and performs the weddings. The Chapel in the Pines became so successful that the Luciuses added a reception hall with full kitchen and a cathedral for outdoor ceremonies in 2003. "I sometimes wish we'd built this 20 years ago," Loretta says, "but I am a believer that God sends things to you when the time is right. This wouldn't have worked for us 20 years ago. Now we expect it to take us well into retirement years."

■ ■ ■

Ways to generate advance interest in a new product or service:

■ Keep existing customers up to date on progress.

■ Seek customers' suggestions and input for making the product or service even better.

■ Schedule a party to give a sneak preview.

■ Tease the "coming attraction" in newsletters, brochures, and on your Web site.

■ Hold a contest, such as asking people to name the new product or event.

72.

SPEAK UP TO
FIND NEW CLIENTS

If you are the speaker at an event, you become the
celebrity expert not just another face in the crowd.

■ ■ ■

Supposedly, the greatest fear in business is speaking in public. If
you're serious about marketing your business, remember these three
words: get over it. Public presentations and speeches are valuable marketing tools that help owners of even the smallest businesses stand out. That's
what Melissa Guzzetta discovered when she started a gift basket business.
She went to many networking meetings and had to hone a brief self-introduction. "At first it was uncomfortable," Melissa says, "even though I had
a speech class in college so I wasn't totally inexperienced at public speaking."

Then she accepted a teaching job for a private computer training company. "They put me through rigorous training in presentation skills. They
didn't concentrate on course content, just repeated practice pretending to
teach a class," she says. The longer she taught, the better her public speaking and presentation skills became. Students evaluated the teachers, and
even when Melissa thought she did a terrible job, she still received high
marks. She had to keep those good evaluations to keep her job. She started
attending the annual conventions of the National Speakers Association,
took note of style and techniques of the best speakers, and incorporated
them into her own presentations. She learned to be dynamic and animated,
and not to speak in a monotone or grip the podium.

Those lessons paid off when she started her own training company,
The Computer Tutor in Costa Mesa, California, in 1998. Not only was she
presenting seminars to people who wanted to learn more about using their
computers, she found speaking was a great way to get people to sign up for
her seminars in the first place. "I find that the more I can speak about my
business, the more likely I am to spark people's interest in getting training," Melissa says. "So it helps to have public speaking skills and to deliver the right message, that is, information people can use. I'm not a
naturally good speaker, but I have a passion for what I do."

Melissa gives frequent, free speeches about computer basics to chambers of commerce and other business groups as a way to market Computer Tutor. "I never do a hard sales job in my speeches. I try to teach them something helpful," she says. "Even so, they introduce me and the name of my company. And afterward, people in the audience always come up and want information about my services."

Computer Tutor provides consulting, one-on-one training, and small classes. Her core clients are not in love with technology and computers. Because many such people are intimidated by speakers who use jargon and technical terms, Melissa uses laymen's terms and examples. "Giving speeches gets my name out there, and lets people see me as an authority," Melissa says. "Being a polished speaker adds to that aura of authority. Even if you're good at what you do, you'll undermine your image as an expert if you don't speak well."

■ ■ ■

Tips for turning public speaking into marketing opportunities:

- Select a topic about which you are knowledgeable and one which is of interest to a large number of prospective customers.

- Avoid self-promotion and sales pitches in your speech.

- Research your topic and prepare a presentation that can be customized to as short as 20 minutes or as long as 45 minutes.

- Practice until your delivery is polished.

- Use acting techniques to enliven your presentation.

- Develop helpful handouts. Make sure your name and contact information is on each page.

- Prepare a packet with your biography, a list of speech topics, and a photo to send to groups that are looking for speakers.

- When presenting at an event with several speakers, avoid being the final speaker of the day. (People tend to leave early.)

- Seek feedback from attendees and program chairmen to improve your presentation for the future.

■ Tape your presentation and listen to it to find ways to improve your speech.

73. WHEN TELEPHONE DIRECTORIES WORK

Not every listing in every category in every telephone directory is a winner.

■ ■ ■

When Liz Schmidt started Intelligraphics in Foothill Ranch, California, to provide Web site design, marketing, and graphic design services for companies, she bought a three-line advertisement in the Yellow Pages of the local telephone directory almost as an afterthought. "I would expect that a high-touch service like mine would not get much business from an impersonal listing in this consumer-targeted directory," she says. Instead, the telephone directory has been one of her most consistently successful marketing tools year in and year out. Each year, Intelligraphics gets a half-dozen jobs from the telephone directory ad, and several turn into long-term loyal clients. Liz also has found that many of the businesses at trade associations and networking groups are small; whereas companies that find her through the Yellow Pages tend to be larger ones with larger projects.

Some companies—especially those that do emergency work as well as routine jobs, such as plumbers—must be in local telephone directories. Some categories have so many full-page ads that you must buy the same size or get lost in the crowd. Every year, millions of large and small companies advertise in the Yellow Pages because 97 percent of American homes have at least one copy. A majority of adults check the Yellow Pages for a telephone number at least once and week. Unlike with other advertisements, people have already made a decision to buy a product or service and are using the Yellow Pages just to choose a company. Ma Bell first used yellow-colored pages for the business advertising section of its telephone directories but didn't trademark the name, which has got to be one of the dumbest marketing mistakes in history. Hundreds of publishers sell ads in gold-colored books labeled "Yellow Pages." In fact, the Federal

Trade Commission has warned about scams in which a promoter sells ads but never publishes or distributes the directory. This problem has spread to "Yellow Pages" on the Internet, so it pays to check out the publisher or Web site owner before paying any money for an ad.

Liz found that the headings under which she advertises have few display ads so she gets good results from a four-line ad that includes: her company name, her Web site address, a list of three of her services, and the city and telephone number of her company. "I've played around with different categories over the years, such as computer graphics, writing, advertising agencies," she says. "I've pretty much settled on Web design, which is what I want to emphasize, and graphic design, which is what people look under." Her choice of categories was helped by asking clients where they would look for her company in the Yellow Pages. Liz also uses red for her company name and bold-faced type for her telephone number to stand out among the other listings in her category. Liz also buys listings in several different geographic telephone directories and the regional business-to-business directory. "I always tell my clients to track which directories people use so they know whether an ad is working for them," she says.

"I've noticed three things about the businesses that call me from Yellow Page ads," Liz says. "People like to do business with vendors that are located near them. They don't get out and network much so they don't know other business owners to ask for a referral to a good service provider. And a small investment for a bold listing or color is worth it in terms of attracting clients."

■ ■ ■

How to get the most out of a telephone directory listing:

- Evaluate whether people tend to look for your type of business in a telephone directory.

- Understand that the name "Yellow Pages" is not copyrighted, so good and bad directories can use the name. Investigate a directory before paying any money.

- List under several categories within one book.

- Some types of businesses need large display ads in the Yellow Pages and others don't. Don't waste money if you're in the latter category.

- Highlight in your ad the benefits that set your business apart from competitors.

- Use boldface type and color to stand out.

- Continually track which ads work and which don't. Ask new customers which directory they use or have them give you the number on the ad, which should be different for each ad.

- Annually evaluate whether the Yellow Pages ad brought in enough business to justify the cost.

74. INFOMERCIALS EXPLAIN NEW PRODUCTS

Thirty-minute commercials that emulate television
programs can increase customer acceptance
of a new, unfamiliar product.

■ ■ ■

It wasn't that Ron Murayama wasn't a good dentist. He was. But he also had a creative, inventive side. In the late 1980s, Ron worked with a chemist to develop the first patented over-the-counter tooth bleaching treatment. "The product, called Natural White, was very expensive, plus the word *bleach* sounded caustic and threatening," Ron says. "The product needed a lot more explanation about how it worked and that it was safe." So he decided to try a new form of marketing called an infomercial, a 30-minute commercial made to look like a TV show. His infomercial sold an astounding $50 million of Natural White in three months.

"In those days we used a live audience like watching a talk show," Ron says. In 1989, most viewers didn't know that infomercials were actually long commercials. Now these ads must be labeled as such. Today, these direct response commercials also come in a short form of less than two minutes that can be more effective for products with a low enough price to prompt an impulse purchase. That's why you see so many $19.95 offers. Some fudge by offering the product for five easy payments of $19.95, but that is less effective. If a product is complicated or benefits from being demonstrated in action, the longer version is a better marketing vehicle. "Certain products in certain categories—the sex and greed products—do better in infomercials," Ron says. He includes in those categories cosmetics, exercise equipment, and how-to-get-rich products.

Ron eventually sold Natural White and started another company, Amden Corp. in Irvine, California, to develop an entire oral care system including the Cybersonic electric toothbrush, a flossing tool, a tongue scraper, and a tooth whitening gel. He turned again to infomercials to sell the Cybersonic system. Television actor Robert Urich was hired to be the "guest host." After Urich died, Vanna White from *Wheel of Fortune* became the host. "Celebrities give a lot of credibility to a product," Ron says. "People channel surf, and they will stop momentarily if they recognize the face." The Cybersonic infomercials used no live audience, but did stop people at a shopping mall to try the product.

The Natural White infomercials brought $6 in sales for every $1 paid for television time, a remarkable result. It was so successful that Ron was afraid to tinker with the infomercial. The Cybersonic brought in $2 in sales for every $1 spent, which is still good. Amden sold $100 million of Cybersonic products in the first two years. But Ron has tested slightly different offers for the infomercials to optimize results. It is important to test an infomercial adjusting the offer, the markets in which it is shown, and times of day or days of the week it airs. "It's surprising how cheap air time can be. In small, regional markets we can pay $500 for a half-hour slot, but we don't get thousands of orders," he says. "The only thing we care about is how much we pay for the time and how many orders we get."

Infomercials are a successful way to introduce a new product that people don't understand or want to see in action before they put their money on the line, Ron says. The infomercial benefits carry over when the product eventually sells in stores. Increasingly product packaging states As seen on TV. "People who buy from infomercials are different from retail customers, so one market doesn't cannibalize from the other," Ron says.

■ ■ ■

Important elements of an infomercial:

■ A well-written and edited script

■ Experienced production and post-production crew

■ Graphics, animation, and action

■ Repeated calls to action throughout the show

■ Tests to determine whether the message is getting through, if it is shown in the proper geographic markets, and if it airs in right time slots for target audience

■ A toll-free telephone number *and* a mailing address for customers who distrust giving their credit card information over the telephone

■ A telemarketing company to handle customer orders generated by the infomercial

■ Efficient order fulfillment

■ A process for accepting returned products and paying refunds

75. RADIO COMMERCIALS

Although radio stations target audiences with specific demographics, they reach a general population, so products or services with mass appeal do better with radio marketing.

■ ■ ■

Roger Schlesinger has worked in the real estate and home mortgage industries since the 1970s. In 1997, he decided to try radio commercials to promote his company, Manhattan West, a division of Skyline Funding Company. Although he is based in Sherman Oaks, California, Roger works with customers nationwide. From the beginning, Roger made his radio ads different than the run-of-the-mill commercials. They are like miniprograms. He even has given them a title: The Mortgage Minute with Roger Schlesinger. He does his own commercials rather than hiring an actor, and he makes 18 different commercials a day, rather than repeat one ad for months. He buys time on several different stations and programs, some of which run nationally, so his commercials are on 100 different stations.

Radio can give even small companies low-cost marketing that reaches a general demographic group, such as working, educated adults on political talk radio. Targeting is imprecise because anyone can pick up the broadcast. However, products like mortgages don't have to reach a carefully picked market. All kinds of people buy homes. Because of Roger's real estate background, he knows how to sell, but he decided he wouldn't be a pitchman in his radio commercials. "I educate and inform," Roger says. "I never say, 'I have this great thing you have to buy.' I don't believe in that."

Roger usually has the show's host "interview" him about the latest twist in the ever-changing home mortgage market. Some are live telephone interviews; some are recorded an hour or two in advance. Some hosts treat Roger more like part of the program than a commercial. "I pay for a minute but sometimes I'm on for five minutes just chatting about the economy and interest rates." If interest rates just dropped to 40-year lows, they discuss that. If rates are steady, Roger may explain how to save money with a 15-year mortgage instead of a 30-year loan. If rates are rising, he tells about variable interest rates. Occasionally, Roger talks more about the news than mortgages. When forest fires burned more than 700,000 acres in Southern California in 2003, he urged listeners to call their insurance agents to make sure they had enough coverage to pay off their mortgages if they lost their homes in a fire.

"People say I sound like their uncle who they can call at any time, which they can," Roger says, referring to his office hours that extend to midnight on the East Coast. Roger's commercials always include a toll-free telephone number and the show's host urges people to call right away. Some radio advertisers include a Web address, which can give more information than a 60-second radio spot can. "I get sensational results," Roger says. He needs to make in mortgage revenue at least ten times the cost of his commercials. He always makes 12 to 13 times spending.

However, Roger had to learn to be patient with radio advertising. "The first 90 days my commercials ran I didn't get one call, and then I started getting 15 calls every morning," he says. "You have to be heard for a long time before people call."

■   ■   ■

Keys to successful radio ads:

■ The message must be clear and direct. Use nouns and action verbs in short, simple sentences.

■ Include a toll-free telephone number to contact your company. Repeat it more than once during the commercial.

■ Emulate commercials that run a lot over a long period of time; they're probably working.

■ Adapt your language to your target audience. Teens and business executives don't respond to the same lingo or message.

■ Be entertaining and informative. Be enthusiastic but not annoying.

■ Call for the listener to take action.

PART 9

GROUPS

■ ■ ■

Humans just naturally gather into groups for all sorts of beneficial purposes: security, fun, accomplishment, education, and more. Businesspeople have learned to use this tendency for marketing purposes. Some people shrink from the notion of using membership and participation in nonbusiness groups for business benefits, but it's a natural link. First, the types of groups you frequent convey a message about your interests, strengths, and skills. Second, you have a great deal in common with people in these groups. They learn to like and trust you; you develop similar trust in them. Because marketing envelops everything about you and your business, the groups in which you are active are part of your marketing whether you maximize the connection or not.

The key to using groups for marketing is to show up. You must invest time and effort, even more than money. You must become active to get to know people and for them to know you. If you value the group's purpose, enjoy the other active members, and take pleasure in the type of functions it hosts, you'll consider this involvement worthwhile for personal as well as business reasons. Don't join too many groups. Your participation, your business, or your personal life will suffer.

Another important aspect to marketing through groups is to identify ones in which your potential customers participate as well. You still are likely to have several groups from which to choose, so feel free to choose the one you enjoy. Some of your groups will stage trade shows or expos. Your participation in these events will vary, depending on your marketing goals. But don't ignore them or go overboard without incorporating them into your overall marketing plan.

76. EVALUATE THE BUSINESS VALUE OF NETWORKING GROUPS

There is no lack of places to network. The marketing decision
is which places are best for your business.

■ ■ ■

With 35 years' experience in the aerospace industry, Frank Garza
started his own consulting practice in Phoenix, Arizona, to help small
aerospace and high-technology firms with business development, quality
management systems, and marketing. But first he had to market himself.
He started getting actively involved in industry-related associations, user
groups, and technology conferences. "It is important to be recognized as
an active and contributing participant," Frank says. "Just being a member
and showing up at events and glad-handing does not work."

But Frank also has a limited amount of time for marketing, so he carefully selects the groups with which he gets involved. "Each networking
event needs to be critically evaluated to determine if it is worthwhile," he
explains. "Evaluation needs to include the types of people that attend and
what their objective is. If an event is populated with an inordinate number
of people looking for employment or attempting to sell a product or service, then the value is negligible. The same holds for associations and
organizations."

Most small-business owners recognize themselves in Frank's situation. Even in rural communities, they can find many different types of
events and groups. It's probably healthy to have a few that have nothing
to do with business marketing. But don't kid yourself that socializing is
building the right relationships for effective marketing. Different types of
groups serve different types of personalities or marketing styles. Salespeople do well in leads groups, which limit membership to one person
from each industry and which require members to bring leads to each
other. Service providers, owners of local-only businesses, and professionals build relationships and business through chambers of commerce.
Some people prefer to associate with others in their own industry through
trade associations. Some develop great business relationships at sports
clubs, golf courses, or Christian businessmen's groups.

Frank is right that merely showing up isn't enough. People do business with people they know, and they don't get to know you if you're not actively involved in the group. The time that such involvement requires is the primary reason to select the group carefully. Time is more valuable than money. You can always make more money, but once you have spent the time, it's gone forever.

Groups can change over time, Frank says. He was active in one powerful Internet group during the dot-com boom of the 1990s. It attracted venture capitalists, attorneys, business development officials, and techie types all of whom wanted to network and do business together. After the technology crash, it became a resume shop for out-of-work Web site workers. "An interesting dynamic occurred at that group," he says. "High-level management people refused to attend after a while because they would be inundated by people looking for jobs, rather than being able to build relationships to do business."

■   ■   ■

Tips for choosing groups or activities for effective marketing results:

- Determine whom you want to reach when networking, and then select groups whose members match your target audience.

- Decide what you want to get out of business marketing through groups. Set goals.

- Determine what you can give to a group, as well as what you can get.

- Check out a group before joining to make sure you can be comfortable and effective there.

- Become active in groups you join.

- Reevaluate the groups in which you are active periodically to make sure the relationship and time investment is still valid.

77. FORM YOUR OWN GROUP

If your industry or topic of business interest doesn't
have a local organization for networking and information
sharing, create one yourself.

■ ■ ■

Gene Scott was a manager at aerospace manufacturer Rockwell International and fledgling entrepreneur starting a patent search company in the late 1980s when a friend and fellow engineer invited him to the first meeting of a new support group for inventors. Gene went to show his support, and the friend announced that he wouldn't be the group's president. "A dozen of us looked at each other, and before I knew it, they made me president," Gene laughs.

The group was first a local chapter of a national group called Inventors Network and then separated into an independent, nonprofit organization called Inventors Forum in Southern California. The association held monthly public meetings with experts speaking about marketing, licensing, or patent protections. Then members met in private sessions once a month to share their inventions and advice. They signed nondisclosure agreements to protect the ideas shared in the private meetings. Membership grew quickly to several hundred inventors and business service providers and experts. "It was a lot of blood and sweat, but over time the audience, and later the entire business venture community, came to recognize my name, face, and capabilities," Gene says.

He eventually changed his patent search firm, Macro Search, to Patent Law & Venture Group in Costa Mesa, California, after he earned his law degree and passed the patent bar exam. Over the years Gene has prepared for himself and others more than a thousand patents. "I was surprised that Inventors Forum worked so well establishing my legal practice in record time," he says.

A nonprofit group like Inventors Forum can help your marketing as well as others' marketing. As in other clubs and organizations, members who become active can demonstrate their work ethic, expertise, and professional strengths. By forming a niche group, you hope you are attracting your most likely customers. Some of the people who helped establish

Inventors Forum owned firms that provide business services. They hoped that by helping inventors create companies, the service providers would be creating future clients, Gene says. But many inventors don't form companies.

A specialty business association like Inventors Forum is no snap to get started, Gene says. First, a core of interested and committed people must identify a niche not filled by other groups. If one exists, you're probably better off just getting active in the established organization. "As in any sort of start-up, you have to be the master who brings in the disciples for your idea," Gene says. "Then others come around and want to help as they see the potential and early signs of success." Broad involvement is even more important with a nonprofit group than for a business. As a group grows, the founder must learn to delegate and involve members or he will burn out and the organization will struggle and eventually die. The group needs membership, community recognition and acceptance, and institutional sponsorship if it is to provide a marketing benefit to member businesses. "I did benefit from Inventors Forum, but it was lopsided in terms of the time I spent. I started with zero," Gene says. "Macro Search took off and was doing well too. I was having so much fun."

■ ■ ■

Basics of a successful trade association:

- Leaders with experience in the industry or subject matter

- A well-defined mission and purpose

- A core of active members

- Services that professionals in the industry or trade will support

- A Web site

- Opportunities for information sharing and networking, such as monthly meetings, a newsletter, or an electronic publication

- Quality ancillary products and services or sponsorships to help support the group financially

- Leaders who are willing to put in long hours to establish and grow the group

78. IT DOESN'T HAVE TO BE BUSINESS

Successful business owners should be networking
everywhere, not just at business clubs.

■ ■ ■

When Donna Fagan started her own certified public accounting
practice in Prescott, Arizona, she knew she needed to network to develop
her clientele. But she didn't jump into the nearest leads group or chamber
of commerce. She accepted an invitation to be treasurer of the Yavapai
Symphony Association, a position she held for seven years. Art and music
are personal interests for Donna so her participation was enjoyable as well
as an opportunity to market to other civic and business leaders. Within a
few years, half her fellow board members were clients. But like other networking and business development activities, participation in civic and
charitable groups takes time. "You have to devote a sufficient amount of
time to the job to impress everyone and gain their confidence," Donna
says. "It seemed like it took a while for the first few clients to call."

After the Symphony Association experience, Donna was treasurer for
the Prescott Fine Arts Association, whose members ranged from starving
artists to newspaper editors and lawyers. "It seemed like I was always
asked to be treasurer of organizations because I am a CPA and because it
seems to be a difficult position to get volunteers to do," she says. "Most
people are intimated by handling money and filing income tax returns."
Combining professional skill with personal interest is a strong marketing
technique for Donna. People who saw her in action in civic groups appreciated her hard work, reliability, competence, and caring personality. So
when they needed an accountant for their personal or business accounts,
they remembered Donna. "I can be a rather shy person," she says, "so
more aggressive marketing strategies were not my style."

Donna doesn't always pursue clients from among the members of
groups to which she belongs, such as a women's social group. "It can hurt
your relationships if the business doesn't work out well," she says, "but
the relationships have been good for business referrals."

Donna also has found other ways to serve her charitable groups and clients. "Teaching classes and giving speeches for various organizations are also good ways to get clients," she says. "This is especially true if you have specialized clients. For example, I have a lot of fire districts as clients, and I did a free class for their statewide fire association. When they need information, they tend to turn to me as a resource."

Donna has gained far more than clients from her civic groups. "When I joined the symphony board, I was 32 and quite naive," she recalls. "The president, an 80-year-old woman, took me under her wing. As I observed how she did things, the way she treated people, followed up on matters, and handled conflicts, I found that I learned so much that would have taken years to learn if I had to learn them on my own. Another benefit of joining these organizations is that I get to associate with many talented people."

■ ■ ■

Finding nonbusiness groups for marketing:

- Consider your hobbies or nonbusiness skills, such as music or sports.

- Look at the ways you enjoy spending leisure time.

- Think of your five best customers. Where do they spend leisure time?

- Be creative. Think of groups or charities that can use your skills.

- Avoid selling at meetings or to other members, but still let them know about your business, products, and services.

- Enjoy yourself. People are attracted to enthusiastic, fun-to-be-with people.

- Give more than you expect to receive. The benefits you receive will surprise you.

79. CHAMBER OF COMMERCE SUITS THE LOCAL BUSINESS

When your products or services sell in a local geographic area, the local business group can be the most effective place to find customers and referral sources.

■ ■ ■

Bob Richardson has owned two Southern California businesses since 1980: Mr. Pet Dog Grooming and Supplies and RWR Marketing & Graphic Design, and both have thrived thanks to the Fountain Valley Chamber of Commerce. RWR isn't even located in Fountain Valley, but Bob sticks with that chamber because he's comfortable with fellow members and those long-standing relationships enabled him to smoothly transition from one industry to another. Mr. Pet drew from a small geographic radius. RWR works with small businesses. Both demographics represent strengths of chambers of commerce. Most chamber members have businesses in the town or nearby, and the vast majority own small businesses.

"My strategy initially was to go where small-business people gather on a regular basis. That was the chamber of commerce," Bob says. "I can trace every one of my clients today—they're worldwide—back to the Fountain Valley Chamber of Commerce." A chamber member hired Bob to do a logo for a client company, which later partnered with a New Zealand company to import wine. They hired Bob to do the wine label. A chamber friend referred Bob to a computer consultant who in turn referred him to a client that provides transportation to the garment industry. The transportation firm is still one of Bob's clients, and so it goes through his list of 50 clients.

Chambers have different personalities, so check them out before joining, Bob suggests. He tried other chambers and leads groups. Some chambers made him feel like a perpetual stranger; leads groups brought one-time jobs but no lasting clients. Some chambers are dynamic and active, drawing in influential community members, and making a difference in local politics. Others are more like small, closed clubs. The dynamic groups are more likely to be good marketing locations to enhance a business reputation and attract strong and long-term client relationships.

Using the chamber as his only marketing venue, Bob stresses the importance of active involvement. He attends every luncheon and mixer, most of the business expos, and some of the member grand openings. "I'm everywhere all the time to try and make sure I am at the right place at the right time," Bob says. "People remember me. We talk business, but I don't sell my business. I'm mainly building relationships." He has been on the board of directors twice. Although he's never been in the chamber's greeting group called Ambassadors, he makes a point of welcoming every visitor at every meeting and introducing them to others. "Being an officer helps a lot and introduces you to more people in a shorter period," he says. "Making new people feel at home helps them remember me in the future." He estimates that he has done work for about 30 percent of the chamber members who show up regularly at various events and has received referrals from another 15 percent. That's a good payback for the investment of five to ten hours a month.

■   ■   ■

Getting the most out of chamber of commerce participation:

- Attend most of the events.

- Make it a point to meet people and develop strong personal relationships.

- Avoid the hard sell.

- Read the chamber's publications and acknowledge those whose business appears in print.

- List your business in the chamber's directory and Web site.

- Participate in committees and activities.

- Join chamber trade missions to other locations.

- Host networking events at your place of business.

- Join a special-interest committee. If your chamber doesn't have one to match your interest, form one.

- Offer your products and services to fellow chamber members at a discount and do business with other chamber companies.

80. TRADE SHOW MARKETING

Not every trade show, even with huge attendance,
is a good market for your business.
Targeting is important.

■   ■   ■

When Marla Silva started her promotional products company, Marla's Mania in Monarch Beach, California, she exhibited in at least four trade shows a year. It was a painful—as in sore feet from standing all day—but profitable education. Choosing the right trade show is the most important factor in trade show exhibiting, and the right show isn't necessarily the biggest, Marla says. "I don't just look at a show flier and decide to exhibit," she says. First, Marla wants to know if the attendees are likely purchasers of give-away products with their company name, or logo on them, which are what Marla's Mania supplies. That usually means she's looking to meet business decision makers. She often attends trade association meetings before deciding whether the membership is compatible with her business. Second, she wants to know a show's history, such as past attendance, percentage of returning exhibitors, and how the show is promoted. "If they've had even one previous show, they have a track record and should be able to give me statistics." Third, she looks for trade shows that limit the number of exhibitors in each business category. "I've been to shows where 11 of the 70 exhibitors were my competitors," she says.

Marla also learned the hard way to demand a good location for her booth. She wants to be next to the food concession or the bar. The end of an aisle is also good. The price of the exhibit space is a factor, but sometimes an inexpensive show is more costly because it results in fewer contacts and less business in the long run. Marla has found that local or regional trade shows bring her a better return on investment than national events because national shows often involve additional travel, hotel, and meal expenses. Also, if they win her clients who are on the other side of the country, she spends extra time and money reassuring them, which hasn't been her experience with clients in her region. Still, making instant sales has never been Marla's goal at trade shows. "Too many people judge a show on immediate response or how many business cards they collect," she says. "I never wanted to make a sale right away. I wanted people to remember me."

Marla advocates contests at a show as long as they are unusual, have a good prize, and benefit the exhibitor. For one client, an engineering company, she created a contest using the firm's aerial photo of a large project it had built. Booth visitors had to guess the cubic yards that had been moved in the construction, writing their guess on the back of their business cards.

The simplest tool for standing out in the trade show crowd, Marla says, is to show an interest in visitors to her booth, to learn more about their businesses so that she can envision ways her company can help them, and to lay the groundwork for follow-up contacts later. "People will come up and say, 'I don't use ad specialties,' and I'll say, 'That's OK, I want to give you a gift,'" Marla says. "Then I tell them they're obligated not to throw away my business card and not to forget me. It works." To be memorable in the midst of flashy signs, tubs of free candy, and colorful exhibits, Marla used to dress up like a clown for trade shows. She also put a color photo of herself in clown garb on her first business cards. It helps that she has a vivacious personality that captivates strangers. "It was amazing to me. People would call three years later because they had kept my card and remembered the clown lady," she says.

■　■　■

How to get your money's worth from trade show exhibiting:

- Carefully select trade shows in which to exhibit.

- Pick the best location, if allowed.

- If you exhibit in more than two shows a year, it's more cost effective to invest in booth displays and elements rather than leasing them.

- Strive to create a booth that can be assembled in less than 30 minutes without special tools.

- Determine your goals before the show starts.

- Remember booth etiquette: Don't sit down, don't eat at the booth, don't talk to other members of your team. You are there for the attendees.

- Qualify visitors before giving them anything or entering them in your contest.

- Consider offering "show only" sales prices rather than giveaways as a means for qualifying visitors.

81. THE VALUE OF SHOWING UP

When working in a niche industry, there's more to marketing at trade shows and events than sitting at an exhibit booth.

■ ■ ■

Since 1983, Bob Banka has collected and sold photographs and drawings of aircraft for model airplane enthusiasts and full-size aircraft restorers. His company, Bob's Aircraft Documentation in Costa Mesa, California, has virtually cornered the market on this sliver of a niche. He owns the world's largest commercial collection of aircraft photos and drawings. But Bob's reputation as the go-to guy for reasonably priced information about airplane authenticity didn't just happen. He has spent years attending trade shows and events for model airplanes all over the country. "I would ask to be introduced to the manufacturers of airplane kits," he says. "I contacted the editors and columnists of magazines in my field and offered free samples and information. If they were going to review a kit, I offered any documentation they want."

Initially, he was the new guy, an outsider, who had to prove his knowledge and worth. "It took a while to get exposure because initially they ignored me," Bob says. "But after a few years of showing up, they got to know my name, and now they seek me out at these events."

Bob works in a niche industry where everyone knows each other. That is a blessing if you are ethical and competent. It's a curse if you make continual mistakes and don't deliver on your promises. By showing up continually, Bob has developed relationships with the representatives of every model airplane publication. They quote him and use his information. He always writes a thank you note for using his name in a story. "I've really worked at building a reputation and making myself known," he says.

The model airplane industry also sponsors hundreds of events, competitions, and "fun flys," in addition to trade shows. In the early years, Bob also attended many of these events—and still goes to the major ones—but eventually got weary of carrying samples of his collection of more than 500,000 aircraft photos. Once you establish your reputation, you don't have to attend every single event, he says. Still, Bob provides prizes for many events. Some event organizers ask him to be a judge of various competitions. "I went to visit a friend of mine from high school in Dayton, Ohio. He said everyone in his club was impressed that he knew Bob Banka," Bob laughs. "Everyone seems to know my name mainly because I've been at all these events and shows all these years."

■ ■ ■

Getting the most out of industry events:

- Get around and meet event organizers, industry leaders, customers, and trade publication reporters and editors.

- Make a list of a few key experts you want to meet and cultivate.

- Talk to people while you are in the food line or waiting for a seminar or event to start.

- Seek out trade reporters and make them aware of your company.

- Develop your reputation as an expert and industry leader in your own right.

- After you've established your reputation, be generous with your time to newcomers.

- Donate products for door prizes.

- Volunteer to give workshops during the trade show or to judge a contest.

- Calculate how many business cards you will need. Take twice that amount.

- Show up consistently and regularly.

82. LEVERAGE CHARITABLE CONTRIBUTIONS

Donations of time and money should reflect the values
of your company, which is a valuable message to
send to customers and the public.

■ ■ ■

For Meg Waters, partner in the public relations firm of Waters and Faubel in Lake Forest, California, contributions to charities, political candidates, and causes are a natural part of business. "Most companies want to donate to causes their owners believe in; it's not self-serving," Meg says. But Waters and Faubel's choice of beneficiaries tells clients, employees, and the community a great deal about the firm and impacts its image. The giving can even impact referrals and work that comes to the business. "If you align yourself with causes that clients care about, it shows you are 'with them,'" Meg says.

The business ought to check out any charity or political cause before making a donation, not just to verify its legitimacy—although that is important—but also to understand its purpose and how it spends its money. Some charities are more efficient with their money, putting a much higher percentage of donations toward good works than administration or raising more money.

Waters and Faubel does a great deal of public relations work on political issues and election campaigns. "You can't play in the political world without contributions," Meg says. "We like to be bipartisan because we believe in coalition building."

But many of the firm's donations are to charities. The firm does work for foster care agencies and the Alzheimer's association. Meg, whose grandmother had dementia, is on the board of the Alzheimer's association because it is personally meaningful to her. However, she acknowledges that committee participation or meeting at a charity fund-raiser is a good introduction to influential people from the community. "If you're on the host committee for a fund-raiser for a good cause, that gets your name out there in the community more than if you buy an ad in the event program," she says.

Meg also involves her clients in her charity work. If she buys tickets to a charity event or a table at a fund-raising banquet, she invites the clients who care about that cause. "It's another way to bond with a client," she says.

Waters and Faubel doesn't set aside a set dollar amount to give to charities because its income can fluctuate greatly from month to month. Instead, the partners look at the amount of money left over at the end of a month. They also donate their time and work, "but frankly, I try not to," Meg says. "It's hard to define how much is enough. Charities expect more work because they don't know your billing rate."

A company should develop a policy or criteria for charitable giving that coincide with business goals, she says. Otherwise the giving is all over the place and time serving on committees interferes with keeping the business going. Still, it's hard to be cut and dried about donations. "It has to be somewhat from your heart and somewhat from your head," Meg says.

■ ■ ■

Tips for charitable giving:

- Develop a policy about giving that is in line with your ethics, corporate goals, and financial ability to deliver what you promise.

- Learn about a charity's goals and needs before giving to that charity to make sure they align with your goals.

- Verify a charity's legitimacy before contributing.

- Select causes important to your customers or employees.

- Set a budget for charitable giving.

- Review your giving annually.

PART 10

STAND OUT

■ ■ ■

The marketplace is crowded with products, services, screaming messages, and pulsating promises. How can you possibly stand out from your competitors? Little things, such as your business cards and brief self-introductions, done consistently and well, add up to strong impressions over time. Your message—whether a gripping history or unique element—can provide a framework for your company's entire image and marketing plan. If your company, product, or service lacks a natural element that differentiates you from competitors, create one. While you're at it, make it as spectacular and forceful as possible. Why bother with a meager point of difference?

It is rare that a company or product is an attention grabber from the beginning. In fact, those that command instant attention frequently lack staying power. Persistence in quality is a valuable marketing habit. So are uniformity and regularity. A message flashed once is forgettable. A message repeated becomes part of your image. The element of time works in favor of the enduring company. It's hard to stand out if you're no longer in business.

83. THE POWER OF A COMPELLING STORY

An enthralling story can't compensate for a weak
product or service, but it can be the plus that
propels your company to success.

■ ■ ■

In 1997, Lisa Ristow's 12-month-old son, Charlie, was diagnosed with Duchenne's muscular dystrophy, for which no cure is known. Doctors said the gregarious, brunette toddler would gradually lose the use of his muscles. Most likely he would not live until his 20th birthday. Lisa and her mother, Shirley Jock, brainstormed to find ways to raise money for medical research. They hit on the idea of founding a company to make quality cologne for little boys and contribute a portion of profits to Duchenne's research. How appropriate. Duchenne's is a boy's disease. Lisa had no idea how to create such a product, let alone build a company to market it. But she couldn't shake the idea. "God put it on my heart that this was it," she says.

She and husband, Bill, launched My Very Own Inc., from the kitchen table in their Yorba Linda, California, home to develop a line of colognes for both boys and girls. The products are carried in stores nationwide, including Nordstrom department stores. At first, Lisa wanted to sell only boys' colognes with rough and tumble names like Touchdown, but the Nordstrom buyers persuaded her that My Very Own would have higher sales if it created a girls product line too. She added colognes and lotions in scents like Butterfly Kisses in 2000.

The captivating story of Charlie is a marketing bonanza that many companies don't have. Entrepreneurs must not fabricate a riveting tale in hopes of capturing the sympathy market. But companies that start from the heart and grow on the founder's touching dream shouldn't shy away from sharing the motivation that makes the company and its products or services special.

"We knew from the beginning the product had to stand on its own without Charlie's story," Lisa says. "It had to be a quality product with a large market. I never cut corners. Even if I told people, 'This is for research,' they wouldn't buy it unless it was a good product." During her first sales call to Nordstrom, Lisa didn't even tell the buyers about Charlie. She presented statistics about the demographics of the market. She stressed the quality of the product. Still, Charlie's story did make a difference. The buyers later told Lisa that they liked the product line from her initial presentation, but when she told them the story behind the product, it clinched the deal.

Lisa has made in-person presentations to Nordstrom's fragrance department sales personnel. The story has made them strongly supportive in marketing the product the customers. Still, the business had to be more than a story. In the beginning, Lisa studied perfumes, their market, the demographics of children's products, and most-likely buyers (it turned out to be grandmothers). She bought essential oils and tried to mix her own colognes. She sought help with business structure and marketing from the Service Corps of Retired Executives. She created My Very Own as a for-profit S corporation and Love Charlie Inc. as a nonprofit entity. Until startup debts are paid off, a percentage of gross receipts go the nonprofit, which channels the money to Duchenne's research. After that, all profits will go to medical research. The small company has contributed hundreds of thousands of dollars for Duchenne's research.

My Very Own sells through a Web site (http://www.lovecharlie.com), as well as through department and specialty stores. The story behind the company is online too, and Lisa acknowledges that Charlie is probably the company's best salesman. But even his story wouldn't bring long-term profitability without a solid business plan and quality products. "God started this project and he won't allow it to fail," she says. "I wanted to know that Charlie's life was for a reason."

■ ■ ■

Elements of a compelling business story:

- A human factor with which the listener can relate or empathize

- A sense of altruism, not just that you're in it for the buck

- The issues that are compelling have a sincere and direct connection with the business

- The story informs or affects a large audience

84. SIGNS POINT THE WAY

A business sign should get your marketing
message across from a distance.

■ ■ ■

Don't tell Ted Hustead that a business doesn't need a sign. His family business, Wall Drug in Wall, South Dakota, has depended on signs since the 1930s. The signs have even become part of Wall Drug's brand. It all started with Ted's grandmother Dorothy on a blistering July day in 1937. The drug store was empty, as it was most days. Wall was in the middle of nowhere. But it was on the way to such tourist attractions as Mount Rushmore, the Black Hills, and Yellowstone National Park. Dorothy heard the traffic rumbling past on Route 16 and she got an idea. How about a little sign on the highway offering free ice water, she proposed to her husband/ pharmacist whose name was also Ted. Ted thought it was silly but worth a try for the struggling business. He and Dorothy lettered onto 12-by-36-inch boards the poem: Get a soda / Get a root beer / Turn next corner / Just as near / To Highway 16 and 14 / Free Ice Water / Wall Drug. He spaced the signs along the highway so people could read them as they drove past. By the time he finished putting up the last one and drove back to the store, customers were already coming in for free ice water. Often they'd buy ice cream or other items from the 1,200-square-foot drug store.

Signs became a staple of Wall Drug marketing. Ted started putting up signs and billboards all over South Dakota and into Minnesota and Wyoming. During World War II, American soldiers put up Wall Drug signs all over Europe. "We were kind of an institution so people loved to advertise for us," says grandson Ted. "They'd take their photo alongside their sign at their barracks and send it to us." While on vacation in England, grandfather Ted thought it would be a good idea to put up a Wall Drug poster in the London subway: "5,160 miles to Wall Drug." Several British newspapers and the BBC television network ran stories about Wall Drug. A Wall Drug sign along the Amsterdam canal still exists.

Today, Wall Drug still has 185 billboards. It pays customers $5 for every clever slogan used on a sign. Wall Drug gives away 14,000 little signs and 8,000 big signs annually to customers. The store's walls are covered with snapshots of Wall Drug signs all over the world including Moscow, Russia, and the South Pole. The signs have prompted priceless publicity through hundreds of newspaper and magazine articles. When the I-90 freeway went in, the Wall signs remained. Despite legal restrictions on roadside signs, Wall has managed to retain many of its signs. "Roadside promotions are still a big part of our marketing plan," says grandson Ted, who runs Wall Drug with his brother Rick.

Bill expanded Wall Drug into a 75,000-square-foot tourist attraction with Western art, animated attractions, dozens of shops, and a cowboy orchestra. The town of Wall has about 800 residents, but during the summer Wall Drug gets 10,000 customers a day. Wall Drug now has five entrances, each with a sign. "Signs put us on the map and continue to help us in advertising," Ted says. "More important, they're part of who we are, our brand."

■ ■ ■

Ways to make a sign stand out:

- Location is key. If laws and landlord rules permit, place the sign high and on the street.

- Keep it short and to the point. Use simple fonts.

- Bold colors—yellow on blue background or red on white background—are eye-catching.

- Lighted signs, if allowed, also stand out.

- Avoid confusing or rude messages.

- Letters should be at least two inches high if viewers are within 50 feet, three feet tall if viewers are 1,000 feet away.

85.   BE UNIQUE

When the type of business you own is common, you can still
stand out by creating ways to make it one of a kind.

■ ■ ■

Chutter General Store is a candy store in Littleton, New Hampshire. America must have more candy stores than towns. But Chutter is the only candy store that has been certified by the *Guinness Book of World Records* as the World's Longest Candy Counter. The 111-foot, 11¾-inch, three-tiered counter is one continuous shelf that runs the length of a side wall in a Main Street landmark building named for Frederick George Chutter, part dry goods salesman, part minister. Carol and Mike Hamilton used Chutter's name when they opened the business in 1995 because his name was on the eaves of the building when they bought it.

The store itself was a dream come true for Carol Hamilton. She cherishes childhood memories of spending her quarter weekly allowance on penny candy at the country store in her hometown of Milton Mills, New Hampshire. Everyone, including Mike, said a candy store couldn't be successful in this era. "We sell penny candy by the piece. You don't get what you don't want," explains Mike. Sixty flavors do sell for a penny per piece. Chutter started with 30 jars of candy and kept adding. When the Hamiltons bought out their business partners in the building, they thought a certifiable world record could be a great marketing plus for the candy store. "I went to the bank to borrow money to build the longest counter in the world, and the banker said, 'Are you crazy?'" Mike says. "They fought me, but they finally gave in." The resulting counter has 700 one-gallon glass jars of candy from Blue Raspberry Frooties and Gobstoppers for a penny apiece to Mint Humbugs for 15 cents and sugar-free Starlight Mints for a dime. "You can't do that and survive if you're not unique, if you're just like every other gift shop," Mike says.

That's why the *Guinness Book of World Records* was important. But getting the loan to build the counter was easier than persuading Guinness to certify it. Chutter's Web master, Daniel Hickey, started the quest at Guinness's Stamford, Connecticut, office in 1999. "They get 15,000 requests a year; they didn't want to open a new category," Mike says. The

Stamford office closed, so Mike started dealing with Guinness's London headquarters. Guinness started asking some questions about the Chutter's candy counter, such as length and whether it was one continuous piece. Guinness kept asking for more photos and more proof. Mike had to enlist the help of local attorneys to draft an affidavit about the counter's length. A local television news crew from WMUR Channel 9 came to the store to do a feature about the candy counter. Hamilton knew the professional coverage would impress the Guinness judges, so he sent a copy of the news spot. "Constantly hounding them helped," Mike adds. After eleven months, Guinness proclaimed the Chutter's candy counter the longest in the world in March 2001.

Such a designation by an organization as well known as Guinness is a huge marketing tool, Mike says. The name hangs on a banner on Main Street over the store's front entrance. "I call it the little candy counter that could," Mike says. "We used to get candy deliveries by UPS three or four boxes at a time. Now we get tractor trailer loads."

■ ■ ■

Ways you might make your business unique:

■ House it in an unusual or landmark building.

■ Seek to set a record with something related to the business.

■ Apply for recognition from a well-known entity.

■ Stock one-of-a-kind merchandise.

■ Establish an unheard-of means of selling your products.

86. PACKAGING THAT OPENS WALLETS

With just seconds to capture busy shoppers' attention,
packaging must stand out and still answer questions
and objections in order to induce the sale.

■ ■ ■

Lindy and Scott Brownsberger wanted to create a line of interactive, multimedia stuffed toys that would "edu-tain" young children. To differentiate their value-added toys from the thousands of stuffed animals on the market, the couple teamed up with zoos and animal sanctuaries to use some of their real-life wild animals as models for the interactive toys. The results are Jean the Chimpanzee, Rachel the Kangaroo, and Kobar the Koala from the Los Angeles Zoo; and Jill the Leopard, Timbo the Elephant, and Leo the Lion from Shambala animal sanctuary. These toys can be "adopted," not merely purchased, from Planet Rascals, based in California. Each soft toy comes with a personalized adoption certificate and CD-ROM of information about the real animal, photos and video clips, games, and animation. The children can also log on to PlanetRascals.com for more interactive games and information about their adopted pets.

But having differentiated the Rascals from plain stuffed toys, the Brownsbergers needed packaging that would grab shoppers' attention and explain why these toys are so special. "I can't believe how important the packaging is," Lindy says. "If the packaging isn't exciting and attract attention, we won't make the sale."

Studies have found that consumers make between 70 percent and 85 percent of their buying decisions as they run through the aisles of stores. A product must grab their attention within three seconds or they trot off to look at something else. Furthermore, most retailers have cut staffing to the core. So the packaging must sell the product.

Planet Rascals went through several packaging designs before settling on the current version. A jungle-looking open-front box surrounds the Rascal. Cardboard leaves hang from the top. The buyer can touch the animal and know how cuddly soft it is. The CD-ROM is visible too, so buyers know without reading the label that they are getting more than just a toy.

The package is shipped inside a box with "air holes" and stamped "real-live rascal." "We get such buzz from the packaging," Lindy says. "I have taken it to birthday parties, and people have said, 'Did you get permission to bring that?' It creates such a stir."

Each element was carefully planned, Lindy explains. The original packaging was white, not green, and lacked the die-cut leaves. "We thought the package should simulate the toy's jungle home, but it had to be generic enough for all six animals," she says. "We wanted it to be open so people could feel the softness of the toy. And we wanted to put the CD-ROM in front so it could be seen, but that meant it needed to be secured so it didn't fall out or get stolen."

Packaging needs to explain enough to answer a customer's questions, but the front needs to be relatively uncluttered. "The biggest challenge is getting all the points across to the consumer," Lindy says. "We have so many messages: Planet Rascals gives back to the zoos, the toys are based on real animals, the children adopt the animal, [there are] fun games, [the toys and Web site have] educational aspects. We had to choose what we wanted to get across." The Brownsbergers are most passionate about the educational aspect, but that might not be the most compelling selling point, Lindy says. The Brownsbergers settled on the adoption aspect and the fact that each toy is based on a real animal. The front of the packaging states, "Adopt and Interact with a Real Animal."

If a package's front is compelling enough, consumers will pick it up. At this point, it's important that the sides and back contain enough information to seal the purchase. Planet Rascals' packaging includes full-color photos of all six animals, which promotes additional sales, and all the educational and entertaining aspects of the toy. The shape and die-cuts that make the Planet Rascals packages so attractive to consumers do have a drawback, Lindy says. "The packages can buckle if they're stacked. Still, she believes the packaging is a winner because customers have told her they like the package so much, they keep it rather than throw it away.

■ ■ ■

How to make your package a marketing plus:

■ Create a personality for your product through the package's lettering, photos, and logo.

- Keep it as simple as possible without sacrificing information consumers need to make a buying decision, including features, benefits, instructions about how to use or install, any cautions, and such details as "batteries not included."

- Use color to attract attention and create a mood.

- Similar packaging for all your products will help build your brand.

- Photos of the product in use can cinch the sale.

87. A BUSINESS CARD THAT STANDS OUT

The business card is one of the oldest and most
basic tools of marketing, yet there are ways to make
even this item noticeable in a stack of cards.

■ ■ ■

When Mary Louise Brozena started her business All Educational Audiology Resource & Services—All E.A.R.S. for short—she envisioned taking her hearing test services in a mobile laboratory to the schools around her Portsmouth, New Hampshire, home. For her business card, she designed one to look roughly like a school bus, but light pink instead of yellow. The bus's "passenger area" is a tab that sticks up if the card is inserted in a Rolodex file. "I believe my catchy business card has proven to be very successful," Mary Louise says. "Because it is a stand-out design, it is memorable and effective in bringing me clients."

Business cards are perhaps the least appreciated marketing tools in the world. Yet they often are the first impression a business makes on potential customers. If you have a service business and go to clients' locations, your card is the only and lasting image they have of the business. These two-by-three-and-a-half-inch cards come in astounding variety. Some are colorful or bear photographs. Some have folding parts or holes. They're made of thick designer paper, plastic, or even wood. There are no rules. Just go on the Internet and search for "unusual business cards," and you'll have access to more than a half-million Web sites full of examples. But fancy or plain, crowded with information or just a name and phone number, the card's purpose is to bring in business. Those that do are great marketing tools, no matter what design experts think.

Even though All E.A.R.S. has evolved without the mobile hearing lab, the bus outline still gets across the idea that Mary Louise specializes is helping schools work with deaf children. This special design was expensive initially, she says, because she had to pay for a die cut that drove the price up to $1 per card. But reorders cost pennies each, so the set-up cost diminishes over time and use of the cards.

Many of Mary Louise's colleagues work in clinics, so they consider her a resource rather than a competitor. "In fact, they are my best referral sources," Mary Louise says. "They keep a stack of my business cards, and when they have a patient who can use my services, they give them my card."

Mary Louise stresses the importance of being generous in giving out your business card. She has handed out about 2,000 in four years although hers is a narrow niche. "I market to special education directors, parents, speech pathologists, and teachers of the deaf," Mary Louise says. "I just have to get my business cards into a handful of decision makers' hands." Still, she never knows when she might encounter the parent of a deaf child or a teacher, so she carries her business cards with her everywhere and keeps spare cards in her car. When she gives out her cards, she always gives two. "If I give them to a parent, the second card always winds up at the school," Mary Louise explains.

■ ■ ■

Ways to make your business card distinctive:

- Make the size larger, longer, or smaller than the standard 2-by-3-and-a-half-inch version.

- Change the color—the most commonly used technique. Different colors convey different images. Full color, though expensive, can be most distinctive.

- Use nonpaper materials such as wood, transparent plastic, or marble.

- Design it in an odd shape such as a circle, vehicle, tri-fold, or knot.

- Make it useful by having a calendar printed on the back, or by using a nail file with contact information printed on it.

- Offer a deal by printing a discount coupon on the card.

- Make it interactive with a game, hologram, or "mood" tester in which the card changes color in a person's hand.

- Add a photo of yourself, or your business or product.

88. YOU'VE ONLY GOT TEN SECONDS

You must have a quick and interesting, yet easy-to-understand self-introduction to capture attention in this hurry-up world.

■ ■ ■

Jack Syage stepped to the microphone to present his company, Syagen Technology Inc. of Tustin, California, to a roomful of professional investors. He was in competition with 14 other entrepreneurs. He had to make a brief presentation about the investment potential of his company that would be attention grabbing and memorable, yet true. "Syagen has developed the technology to detect bombs in baggage at airports," he told the investors and then spent five minutes explaining what his biotechnology company does and why it's a great investment opportunity.

His was voted the top presentation of the evening.

Entrepreneurs find themselves in similar fast-pitch situations all the time: networking groups, an elevator, investor presentations, and more. In this hurry-up age, you have seconds to grab attention before the listener gets off the elevator at the next floor or glances over your shoulder wondering if he knows that guy in the corner wearing the green tie. In the late 1990s, bomb detection work was a secondary market for Syagen Technology. Its high-speed molecular-analysis technology had promising applications in the booming life sciences and biotechnology fields. However, presentations to professional investor groups are especially fast paced,

Jack says. "Initially I'd try to explain the cost of new-drug development and how we can speed up the process etc., but it was too complicated," he says. "So when I'd pitch to investor groups, I'd start with something everyone knew about, bomb detection in luggage. It was so much easier for people to understand."

After September 11, 2001, Syagen's high-speed molecular analysis for bomb detection, and its application for detecting chemical and biological weapons, became highly interesting to the Federal Aviation Administration and U.S. Army, among others. Owners of businesses in other industries rarely have the luxury of the undivided attention of officials trying to stop terrorists. They need that memorable self-introduction—and occasionally three or four different ones—as they market their products and services.

Generally, these micromarketing opportunities must be short, interesting, indicative of the target market, and, if possible, surprising. The person who does computer maintenance says, "We do Windows." The electrician says, "Let me remove your shorts." The muffler shop owner says, "You don't need an appointment with me. I'll hear you coming." The business broker says, "I run an adoption agency for entrepreneurs."

Some people are uncomfortable with self-introductions that are too flip. Others avoid comedy because of their industry. Funeral home directors rarely crack jokes about their business, although many are witty people, and that's OK. If you've branded yourself as a caring, sensitive company, the self-introduction should match, such as "See us for memories that will last an eternity."

Jack doesn't always have to make a fast and memorable impression on behalf of Syagen Technology. When he contacts other companies about potential strategic alliances, he talks with engineers and scientists who understand his technology and give him all the time he needs to explain how Syagen can work with their companies. In such cases, Jack says, he must be careful to be dispassionate and not to oversell Syagen's capabilities.

■   ■   ■

Tips for crafting a memorable self-introduction:

■ Keep it short and crisp.

■ Make it distinctive. Name and company aren't enough.

■ Focus on the benefits for the listener.

■ Make it complete. Humor shouldn't disrupt your meaningful message.

■ Practice. Those snappy sayings that seem off-the-cuff rarely are.

■ Match your personality. If you're not witty, don't force it in a self-introduction.

■ Match your audience. Some groups are fun loving. Others want swift introductions. Others are staid.

89. MEET MY PET PIG

If you're going to adopt an outlandish marketing theme in order to get attention, don't use moderation. Be bold and consistent.

■   ■   ■

After Aralyn Hughes won a pot-bellied pig in a silent auction, the Austin, Texas, Realtor decided to use the 65-pound black and white animal in her marketing. "People said, 'you put that pig on your business card, you're dead. No one will ever buy real estate from you again,'" Aralyn recalls. "I did it anyway." And she did it completely. Not only is a full-body profile of the pig wearing a yellow party hat on the front of Aralyn's business card, but a rear-view photo of the pig named Ara, also called Babe, in a sequined tutu is on the back of the card. Babe is featured prominently on Aralyn's Web site and business stationery. Aralyn has adopted the tag line: Piggish on real estate. She takes Babe to birthday parties for clients and their children. Aralyn also takes Babe on caravans with other agents to view homes that have recently come on the market.

The first year Aralyn put Babe's photo on her card, business increased 20 percent. By incorporating Babe into so many aspects of her marketing, Aralyn has become known as "the pig lady." Many business owners wouldn't want to be known by such a handle, but Aralyn shrugs. "I didn't want to be like everybody else. I wanted to take a risk." The lasting impression with most people is one of fun, not of unattractive habits and hygiene. Aralyn is a vivacious saleswoman who loves people, wears bright colors, and enjoys self-deprecating humor. "I wanted to walk into a room and have everyone say, 'You're the great Realtor.' That didn't happen," she says. "Now, anywhere I go, people ask me what I do for a living, and I say I sell real estate and I market myself with a pig. Immediately they shout, 'I know you! I've heard of you.'"

That kind of memorable image is a tremendous boost in the highly competitive residential real estate industry. People who might not sell their homes for years after meeting Aralyn will remember her when they are ready to make a move. Aralyn believes that one reason the pig works for marketing is because it's unusual. Babe may not be elegant, but she's cute. So many business owners are trying to create an image of professionalism or sophistication that they have a tough time distinguishing themselves from all the other professionals and sophisticates.

Pig marketing works to create that recognizable image for Aralyn that builds her business. It also attracts free publicity that continues to build her reputation as the pig lady. The city of Austin has a contest to identify people "who keep Austin weird." Aralyn was nominated. "I built my client base without the pig," Aralyn says, "but she has definitely enhanced business."

■ ■ ■

Tips for creating a clear and notable marketing tool:

- ■ It should be unusual. If competitors all use blue, you use hot orange.

- ■ It makes a human connection with people.

- ■ It's bold. Forget me-too-ism.

- It should complement your personality without being boring.

- It doesn't have to be ridiculous to have personality.

- It's genuine. It's not just a plastic overlay on your business.

90. CLEVER REMINDERS

Staying in touch with valued sources delivers greater marketing
mileage when it is not dull or routine.

■ ■ ■

Conway Chester owns two office buildings in Southern California
that he leases as executive suites to a variety of short-term and long-term
tenants ranging from business start-ups to branch offices for major corporations. In commercial real estate, landlords come and go, buildings convert
from one use to another, and the space needs of tenants change. So Conway
needs to keep his company, Execuplan, visible and memorable in the minds
of businesspeople who might refer new tenants in need of office space and
accompanying centralized secretarial services and office amenities.

Conway can't count on people remembering Execuplan, even though
it has been leasing executive suites since the 1980s. So he has developed
a series of pun-packed packets in three-by-five-inch plastic bags that he
mails regularly to potential tenants and referral partners. One containing
tiny scissors that bears the label Cut your overhead—survive the slump,
is ideal for slow economic times. One with the familiar blue packet of artificial sweetener says There is NO EQUAL to our SUITE DEALS. The
packet marked We're a Lifesaver for those who need a new office, features a miniature roll of Lifesavers candy. And the one that contains a
plastic insect asks Bugged by your office? You'll be treated like royalty
in an Execuplan Executive Office.

Each packet has the company name and phone number on the clever
label and holds Conway's regular business card along with the Cracker
Jack–like prize. Conway calls these inserts "message amplifiers that help
us stand above the crowd, to be seen as a proprietary entity rather than a
commodity in our industry. What is surprising is that as corny as the con-

cept may seem, it is remembered," he adds. "We have people who will recall receiving one of our candy or other packs years before. It is a surprise when you find out that you've remained in a tiny part of someone's memory that long."

The candy packs were a natural play on words for the office suites Execuplan offers and on its ability to offer greater value and services because Conway owns the buildings, unlike many of his competitors that rent and sublease space in a regular office building. Conway initially handed out the candy packs at networking events, various business associations, and "anywhere I'd meet people who might need or know someone who needs a new or better office set up," he says. Eventually, he started enclosing the message amplifiers in marketing mailings along with a longer letter sometimes promoting Execuplan suites, and other times some other topic of interest to the recipient. The responses to these mailings and handouts have been wide ranging, Conway says. Some call or come in because of the uniqueness of the package and lease a suite. Others pass them along to acquaintances known to be in the market for office space, which is as good as a personal referral. Still others call and want to know where Conway got the little bitty scissors or some other insert. "It is flattering when we have such calls, but it also says that while our idea may be catchy and brought a contact, it wasn't one that produced the desired result of marketing the suites and services we offer," he says.

It is impossible to know the long-term effect, he adds, because some people don't call to schedule a tour until their current lease is up for renewal months or years later. The key is continuing the effort over a long period of time and not falling into staid messages. "If I need to, I'll stand on my head or eat a bug if that's needed to increase awareness of our special suites," Conway laughs.

■　■　■

Clever ways to stay in touch:

- Tiny gifts that tie in to your company name, product, or service

- Daily jokes or thought for the day e-mailed to selected customers and referral partners

- News articles or other useful information of special interest to the recipient

- Party or open house tied to a made-up holiday like National Talk Like a Pirate Day at a costume shop

91. THE WINNING WAY

Awards are not only a good marketing tool. Preparing to win
them improves every part of your business.

■　■　■

Brian Johnson knows firsthand the value of award recognition for his company, Motoring Services Auto Repair, with shops in Richland and Kennewick, Washington. After a local newspaper ran a story and color photo about Motoring Services winning the Gold Award for Mid-Columbia Business of the Year, business increased 40 percent overnight. Awards can bring a business valuable publicity through media coverage, third-party validation of worth, and recognition among peers that can open new opportunities. The mere application process can improve your business, Brian says. Many competitions give invaluable feedback about your business, he explains. "You need that. You need to know what you're doing right and what you're weak at." Motoring Services, which was started by Brian's father in 1979, has had certification from Automobile Association of America, NAPA, and AC Delco almost from the beginning. In 1997, Brian entered his company in *Northwest Motor Magazine*'s hunt for the Northwest Auto Shop of the Year and won. That started a string of competitions and victories that have both improved the company and validated its quality work.

Americans love contests, so there are literally thousands of awards, from ones you win by paying for them to prestigious and highly competitive recognition. Some businesses want to be recognized for their creativity, so they may seek out contests that pay tribute to wackiness. But others steer clear of anything that smacks of frivolity. The competitions that Brian enters focus on quality work, customer satisfaction, community involvement, and employee happiness. In 1997, he entered Motoring Services in the Washington State Quality Award Program, patterned after the prestigious national Malcolm Baldrige National Quality Awards. The WSQA recognizes those organizations that demonstrate commitment to customer satisfaction and continually improving operational performance. "We didn't win, but I entered because it gives you a thorough look at your business," Brian says.

Applications for such awards are so detailed that most business owners won't take the time. That first time, Brian spent 170 hours on his application and knew it wasn't enough. When he applied for the WSQA award in 2000, the feedback and scores from the previous entry helped him improve his business and his application. Wife Patti, who is a business-quality expert and past examiner for the WSQA awards, helped prepare the 2000 application. The pair devoted more than 500 hours to the entry. "You never take the time to look that thoroughly at your business; that part is most valuable," Brian says. Motoring Services won the WSQA award in 2000. Also that year, the company won the Gold Award for Mid-Columbia Business of the Year and South Central Washington Small Business of the Year from the U.S. Small Business Administration. The next year, Motoring Services won the SBA's top prize for the entire state of Washington.

Brian took a break from award submissions in 2001 because he opened the second store in Kennewick. Without applying, he won the national best automotive video commercial for 2002 from the Automotive Services Association. Some awards get more media coverage than others. But Brian uses all of them in his marketing. The company's Web site states on every page: Award winning auto repair and customer service. Brian says, "The recognition is great. You need that for your customers to go out and sell your business to their friends. But you also gain the value of having a look at the company so you can spot areas to improve."

■ ■ ■

Tips for seeking award recognition:

- Find appropriate contests. Contact trade associations, local and national business groups, schools, nonprofit organizations, and skill-based events.

- Look for contests that reward outstanding businesses in an area of your own special interest, such as quality improvement or community service.

- Study criteria for the contests you target.

- Make improvements in your business to be worthy of winning.

- Prepare a top-quality application that reflects the worthiness of your business and respect for the group sponsoring the competition.

- Don't enter just to win. Find other value for your business in the skill or quality being honored.

- If you do win, share the good news with employees, customers, friends, and the media.

PART 11

TACTICS

■ ■ ■

Marketing, as you have read throughout this book, is a coordinated and planned process that encompasses your entire business. This section looks at some specific projects that worked especially well for companies of different sizes and in different industries. Nothing works all the time in every circumstance, but these examples offer you still more projects to try and should stir your own creativity when developing just the right marketing tactic to capture your customers. Remember, marketing should be fun. It should engage you and your customers. Most importantly, it should build up your business. Regardless of what marketing effort you make, continually test, evaluate, and adjust it. Each dollar and minute spent on marketing is precious. Don't waste them. Continual improvement will make marketing increasingly effective and enjoyable.

92. GIVE AWAY SAMPLES

A free example of your handiwork can turn a prospect into a paying customer.

■ ■ ■

In the mid-1970s, Bruce FaBrizio and his father created a cleaner to remove the tannic acid from machinery used to roast coffee beans. They soon discovered that the emerald-colored degreaser worked great on barbecues, floors, stoves, and cars as well as coffee pots. More significant, this cleaner was safer than its toxic competitors. Bruce named it Simple Green and sold $62,000 worth of the cleaner in 1980.

But even a better cleaner has a tough time attracting attention in a product category dominated by giants like Proctor & Gamble. The biggest challenge was getting customers to try Simple Green in the first place. Bruce's company, Sunshine Makers Inc., started handing out one-ounce, clear-plastic packets of Simple Green at stores, trade shows, and other large gatherings of consumers most likely to have something to clean at home or on the job. The company also mailed millions of packets to residences. Bruce wanted to be sure that potential customers received a sample large enough to understand how effective the cleaner was, but not so large that they didn't need to buy a whole bottle. For that reason, industrial customers who were likely to buy Simple Green in five-gallon pails, received samples as large as a gallon. Eventually, consumers received a half-ounce sample in a flatter, foil packet whose product description was easier to read. Sunshine Makers has given away tens of million of samples over the years and continues to use this marketing strategy. It has helped grow sales in excess of $50 million. Surveys prove the value of this technique. More than half of Simple Green customers first learned of the cleaner by receiving a free sample.

Sunshine Makers found another valuable use for its samples: incentives for retailers to stock Simple Green. Every retail customer received individual packets to give to its customers.

Samples are usually associated with products. They help introduce a new product or demonstrate effectiveness better than mere word descriptions. Food manufacturers often find a taste is worth a thousand words.

But service companies can also give samples. Many consultants give a free, one-hour session. Chiropractors may give free shoulder massages at trade shows. Again, the goal is to give a large enough sample to bring customers back for more, with their checkbooks open.

■　■　■

Four keys to effective sampling:

1. Determine the right amount of product or service to give away to prompt a consumer to buy a larger amount.

2. Identify the best way to reach your most-likely customers, such as handing out samples at a specialty store or to targeted groups.

3. Enclose with the sample adequate information to differentiate it from competitors.

4. Make it easy for recipients of free samples to buy. If giving out samples in person, have full-sized products on hand to sell. If mailing samples, enclose a coupon.

93. AN EVENTFUL INTRODUCTION TO THE MARKET

An attention-grabbing event can make your company
name memorable when entering a new market.

■　■　■

Millions of teenagers and young women recognize the name Wet Seal as a nationwide chain of almost 500 contemporary, junior women's clothing stores. But a few years ago, when Wet Seal was starting to grow beyond its bikini-shop roots, few people outside Southern California had ever heard of this retailer. The company was moving into new markets, and then-president Ken Chilvers didn't want potential customers thinking Wet Seal was some circus act. So Wet Seal's public relations firm, Gloria Zigner & Associates, dreamed up a crazy gimmick to introduce the newest store to the college town of Chico, California. Wet Seal sponsored Sealed with a Kiss, an eight-hour kissing marathon.

Wet Seal first had to make sure that kissing contests were legal. They were, but dance marathons, so popular in the 1930s, weren't. Planners dreamed up a few rules and arranged for enough bathrooms and meals. They devised a few activities, such as dancing the hokey pokey and playing paddle ball just to make it tougher for the couples to remain engaged, at the lips, of course. To entice entries, Wet Seal offered female contestants a $1,000 shopping spree and their male kissmates $500 cash. What fun. What publicity in a new market.

What a near disaster.

Such events, which seem so effortless when viewed from the back row, require logistical planning, heavy promotion, and luck to achieve the desired attention and marketing punch. No detail should be left to chance. For Wet Seal's kissathon, thousands of people entered during the weeks before the event. But when company representatives called the entrants a few days before the contest's scheduled date, it was clear most hadn't read the instructions. They merely thought they were entering a prize drawing. The public relations team promoted the dickens out of the kissathon. They spread fliers, posters, entry forms, counter displays, and T-shirts all over town, especially during class registration at the local university. They approached the Top 40 radio station to provide emcees and free on-air promotions. Wet Seal spokesmen took to the airwaves to pump up interest in the contest and prizes, so eventually 20 couples showed up. Every participant signed a liability release. The payoff was big. All three network affiliate television stations and virtually every radio station in the market broadcast stories about the event. The local newspaper ran an article beneath a banner headline plus photos. The publicity not only gave that store a strong opening, it established the name Wet Seal in that market as the hip juniors fashion retailer, not a Barnum & Bailey reject. Attention-grabbing events must match the company image and the targeted market. Wet Seal was promoting its youth orientation. A college town and young female customers were good matches for a kissathon. But even Wet Seal didn't try the event when it opened stores in more diverse markets.

■ ■ ■

Steps for creating an attention-grabbing promotion:

1. Be bold. Customers and media will ignore half-way measures.

2. Match the type of event with your company image and market you want to reach.

3. Check all legalities and obtain any needed permits.

4. Leave no detail to chance.

5. Lavishly promote the event. Bring in media cosponsors, if possible.

---

94. PRIME THE PUMP

Introduce your company and capabilities with quality
information that establishes you as a reliable expert.

■ ■ ■

When Lew Alton started his own investment banking firm, L.H. Alton & Company in the Bay Area of Northern California, he knew that he needed to establish his expertise with institutional investors. People charged with the fiduciary responsibility of wise investing of other people's money have no trust for advisors they don't know. So Lew started building that trust by preparing well-crafted, carefully thought-out and timely research reports on companies in which these pension funds, mutual funds, and others might have an investment interest. These reports had to be information and analysis that these investors didn't have on their own, which would be difficult to produce if Lew didn't know business and investing thoroughly. Over time, Lew published research reports on a thousand public companies. He didn't send every report to every investor. "We got a lot of information about what each institutional investor would buy. They would describe themselves as 'large cap' fund or 'large cap growth' or 'dividend purchasing' company," Lew says. "So we had a good idea of the type of company their investors wanted to buy. We broadcast our reports within that group of investment funds."

While Lew considers these research reports to be the best possible marketing tool in an industry where knowledge is king, he didn't anticipate what a long-range marketing strategy this work would be. The research reports certainly weren't able to jump-start sales. They were more like initial introductions that started a slow and elaborate relationship-building process. "I sent out these reports, and nothing would happen. I literally didn't do any business for six months," Lew recalls. "Eventually, one person called. But then I didn't do any more business for 30 days. Then it was 15 days between deals, then 10 days. Finally, I was getting business every week and then every day. It just took an incredibly long time."

The investment community is built on two fundamental factors: personal relationships and the quality of the service or product produced. Lew now thinks it would have been better in the start-up months to bring into his firm professionals who already had established client relationships with institutional investors. When money is involved, people are even more reluctant than usual to deal with people they don't know. Lacking the established relationships with his client base, Lew needed the research reports to establish the quality of his work and advice. Also in the early stages of business, some of the recipients of Lew's research reports took his information and invested through another investment banker. "That's the nature of the industry," he says. "Eventually the quality of the research and the depth of knowledge demonstrated [in the reports] attracted them to do business with me."

Producing research that was of high quality to impress professional investors is an expensive endeavor. Over time, Lew would be repaid for his expenditure of time and effort through commissions on investment transactions and ultimately through fees involved in helping companies to go public. L.H. Alton & Co. has underwritten public stock offerings for 500 companies.

■ ■ ■

Information products that establish your expertise:

■ White papers

■ Articles in scholarly journals

- Books

- Articles or speeches for respected national trade groups or academic meetings

- Research studies for think tanks, academies, or government agencies

- Opinion articles for quality national publications

- Highly valued reports on a subscriber-only portion of a Web site

95. SEND YOUR MESSAGE TO THE TOP

When you're trying to break through to a highly targeted group
that is difficult to reach, try the curiosity factor.

■ ■ ■

Jim Alampi, chief executive officer and president of Michigan-based Insurance Auto Auctions, had a quandary. His company provided claims processing services and auctioned off vehicles that insurance companies had written off as total losses. Jim wanted to market to his counterparts at the nation's largest insurance companies, such as Allstate and State Farm. These top executives are difficult to reach. But Jim thought a CEO-to-CEO message would be an effective marketing tool . . . if he could just get in the door. "You need to penetrate in a way that is totally unique and different," Jim says.

Jim understood his highly targeted audience because he had dealt with chief executives of various companies for years. It was 1996, and DVDs were new on the consumer market. So Jim prepared a three-minute introductory presentation and burned it onto a DVD. But he didn't rely on the recipients owning a DVD player, understanding how to use it and taking the extra step of actually playing his message. The unfamiliarity factor was one of the pluses of his technique. Also, such a marketing ploy wouldn't be worth the expense for low-priced or low-profit-margin products and services. The automotive salvage industry was huge and growing.

"I bought a dozen portable battery-powered DVD players, loaded my presentation in each and mailed the player and DVD to insurance company CEOs," Jim says. "The enclosed letter merely had instructions on pressing the 'play' button to start the DVD." Even the busiest executives couldn't resist. Virtually every recipient was curious enough to press the play button and spend three minutes watching something from another CEO that described how Insurance Auto Auctions could help his company save money. Jim's letter also told the executive whom to call for an appointment for an account executive to stop by, answer any questions, and pick up the DVD player.

Even Jim was surprised how curious most chief executives are with technology or novel approaches that raise their interest. It, no doubt, helped that the presentation they saw was from the top executive of Insurance Auto Auctions and the company's service was truly valuable to these insurers. "They were all impressed with a new approach," Jim recalls.

Jim is now managing director of Solutions At Work LLC in Farmington Hills, Michigan, and coach to top executives. Some of his clients have tried his DVD introduction with high-level customers they have had difficulty breaking through to in traditional marketing ways. The technology is much better and cheaper now. The strategy continues to work, but it is still difficult for even top executives of mid-sized companies to get face-to-face time with their counterparts in the largest companies, Jim says. The newest technologies and unique approaches that experienced executives haven't seen a dozen times before work best.

■ ■ ■

Tips for reaching that tough audience:

- Narrow the market you want to pursue as tightly as possible.

- Study your target carefully to understand the best "hot button" to push with your marketing.

- Make sure the potential upside financially for your company is worth unique marketing approaches.

- Don't invest in a mere gimmick. It must be a unique or different technology or approach that a highly experienced business person hasn't seen many times.

- Keep it simple. Make it easy to do.

- Give the recipient simple ways to respond to your call for action.

- Follow through and be prepared to act when you connect with your hard-to-impress potential client.

96. A SWEET REMINDER

Small gifts can keep you in customers' minds without violating conflict-of-interest policies or breaking your budget.

■ ■ ■

Small distributors of mundane products like adhesive tape struggle to stand out in the business world. Even a specialist like Tapes II International, a Santa Ana, California, company that prides itself in stocking 150 different tapes from floor-marking strips to copper-lined insulation tape, needs a "here we are" hook. In the late 1990s, the company started putting hard candy in all the boxes shipped by United Parcel Service or Federal Express, says President Patricia Cotton. "My daughter, Elizabeth, worked here even before I bought the company, and the candy was her idea," Patti says.

Elaborate gifts to customers and prospects have fallen out of favor for many reasons, not the least of which is avoidance of any hint of bribes. So many companies of all sizes have developed written conflict-of-interest policies that three-martini lunches and tickets to the opera or Major League Baseball World Series are often unwelcome offerings. The giver who violates such policies risks losing a customer. But small items, like wrapped hard candy, can convey a sweet marketing reminder of your company without setting off alarm bells. Tapes II doesn't send chocolate because it might melt in the shipping boxes. Givers must be careful that the gift doesn't offend, such as wine sent to a recovering alcoholic or a cured ham to an observant Jew. Hard candy is suitable for most people and it isn't perishable. Most important, from a marketing perspective, the candy makes Tapes II memorable, Patti says.

The company's employees receive laudatory comments about the candy almost every day, and the candy has saved more than one business relationship. "There have been many times a customer has called screaming every name in the book because an order did not arrive as we promised. We always request that the customer check with his receiving department and ask if they have opened a box with candy in it. Amazingly enough, the receiving personnel always remember that box, which is instantly located. We get an apology and the entire incident reenforces that we deliver as promised," she laughs.

Tapes II ships worldwide and the candy has become an expected part of each order. "Buyers from California to New York pick up the phone just to let us know their boxes that just arrived didn't have any candy," Patti says. "We apologize and promise to include the candy in the next order. Now at the top of our monthly shopping list is 'shipping candy.'"

■ ■ ■

Tips for planning customer gifts:

- Be mindful of conflict-of-interest policies at client companies.

- Avoid gifts that are inappropriate or offensive.

- Personalize a gift, if possible. Your knowledge of your customer signals that you care.

- A group gift, such as food basket, may be suitable for a client's entire office.

- Establish a tradition so that the gift becomes a memorable part of your company's image with your customers.

97. NEW PRODUCT TIMING

Don't release all your new products at once.
Spread them out to maximize impact and attention.

■ ■ ■

Zack Phillips was 16 when his disappointment with the quality of foreign-made bicycle parts sent him to a machine shop near his Rochester, New York, home. He showed the owners some broken parts and asked if they could make these parts better. The resulting products launched Kink Inc. in 1994. The company now makes about 40 different products and distributes complementary bicycle accessories and parts from other manufacturers. Kink doesn't sell assembled BMX bicycles, but it makes or distributes almost all the parts to build a custom bike.

From the early years, Zack liked to advertise in magazines that specialize in BMX bike riding, and that form of marketing has come to drive the timing of Kink's new products. Any company that wants to grow must continually develop and introduce new products. This habit feeds consumer and retailer interest. "We're working constantly on new products," Zack says. At any given time, "we have half a dozen products behind the scenes that no one knows about."

Initially, Kink did introduce two or three new products in the same month. But to throw too many products on the market at one time would dilute the impact for each product. So Kink spreads out its new-product introductions. The company tries to release eight new products each year, spreading them out so that one comes out every six weeks. "We could have three products come out in one week, but then they get lost in the crowd," Zack explains. "We stretch every dollar of advertising. We focus on one product at a time for maximum effect."

The company wants to have a new product in almost every magazine edition in which it advertises. The company also sends postcards and faxes to its dealers to keep their interest high by focusing on a new product each time. "We also make calls to our dealers, and it helps to have something new to open a conversation with," Zack says. "The first words out of most of our dealers [mouths are] 'Do you have anything new?'"

Kink's typical customer is a boy who has a standard BMX bike who starts upgrading certain parts. He might go to his local bicycle shop and buy Kink handlebars. A few weeks later he adds a seat, and two months later is back for a Kink frame. Kink's professional BMX freestyle team tests the new products and suggests improvements.

"If our team members like our products and the kids see our professionals riding them, they will generally purchase our products," Zack says.

■ ■ ■

Tips for a smooth product introduction:

- Before designing a new product, listen to customers about what they want and why.

- New products should still be within the realm of your company's core expertise.

- Understand the market for the new product, both in terms of most-likely buyers and existing competition.

- Retain the things that made you successful in the first place.

- Adapt the timing for maximum exposure and the focus of both media and customers.

- Time the new product introduction during a slower period in your annual cycle, if possible.

- Don't neglect the core business while trying to focus marketing attention on the new product.

- Resolve any logistical or quality problems before releasing the new product.

98. LOW-COST CONTESTS

Creating a contest with prizes from other small
businesses can offer a win-win situation for the
businesses and fun for customers.

■ ■ ■

Like most start-ups, Basia Christ didn't have much money when she started Marketive Inc., an Aliso Viejo, California, consulting practice specializing in small-business clients. So she started a monthly raffle that would create excitement among clients and prospects, get her name out in the community, and develop relationships with other small businesses. "I asked two other members of the chamber of commerce and one member of my Rotary Club to donate their products or services for prizes," Basia says. First prize was a $100 gift certificate toward using her marketing services. Second prize was $50 worth of advertising specialties products from one of the donors. Third prize was the choice of $25 worth of cosmetics or a gift basket from the other two donors.

Prizes are limited only by the imagination of the donor. Retailers and other product-oriented businesses tend to offer tangible products, but a clothing store might offer free alterations instead. A copy shop might offer free binding with a print order. An accountant might give a free Quick-Books lesson. A copywriter might write a speech. Any company with a Web site can offer a free ad on their site for a month. Basia gave raffle tickets to any likely client she met and to business owners who answered a survey whose information provided market research for her business. The contest was a big hit with both clients and prize donors. The winners redeemed their prizes and almost always bought something else from the donating business. In many cases, they established an ongoing working relationship. "I also follow up to make sure the winners used the prize and get their opinion about the products or services," Basia says. "I then give that feedback to the company that gave the prize, which was another value for them in giving the prize."

Most small-business owners were willing to join the contest as a way to get their name and capabilities in front of new customers, says Basia, who is involved in more areas of the community than most business owners, so her contest reached potential markets many of the prize donors would not find on their own. She started posting monthly contest winners on her Web site, which generated more traffic for her site and more visibility for her company name and capabilities. It also reminded visitors what Marketive Inc. could do for their businesses. The contest creates a community of like-minded people. She has received referrals from people who have been entered into the contest and businesses that have given prizes. They realize they're getting more than just a one-shot introduction; they're actually getting business, Basia says, and people who receive something are more likely to give back and to pass on something of value to others.

■   ■   ■

Create your own contest:

- A retailer can set up a "birthday dart board" divided into sections labeled "10 percent discount," "two for the price of one," etc. On his or her birthday, a customer throws a dart to win a prize.

- Businesses ranging from restaurants to fitness clubs can set out fishbowls. People put in their business cards for a chance to win a lunch or free membership.

- A company can stage a contest for customers to name a new product or service shortly before it is introduced.

- You can fill a large container with pieces of candy. The customer who comes closest to guessing the number of pieces wins one of your products or an hour's worth of services.

99. BE THE CUSTOMER, NOT THE SALESMAN

When you assume responsibility for developing your own
products, your leadership can open dialogue with other
decision makers that being just a salesman cannot.

■ ■ ■

Inventor Eliot Geeting has successfully placed his products on the
market since 1986. Having worked on more than 100 inventions for himself and others, and getting 15 of them to market, Eliot's preferred tactic
is to license the inventions to existing companies. The reason is simple.
These companies already have sales, marketing staffs, budgets, distribution channels, and track records. Why reinvent the wheel?

But finding willing licensees is never easy and sometimes impossible.
In such cases, Eliot doesn't shelve the invention. He takes control to manufacture and market the products himself through his company, Eliot
James Enterprises Inc. in Dana Point, California. That take-charge attitude
can serve valuable marketing purposes. In one such case, Eliot developed
a no-mess applicator for automotive cleaning liquids. "I put a design patent
on it, but my rights weren't that strong," Eliot says. "I approached the makers of various waxes and protective products. They were willing to buy applicators from me, but not license and make them themselves." Eliot
moved forward to manufacture the applicator and decided his sales would
be greater if he packaged his product with complementary products, such
as cleansers or protective liquids. Eliot called companies to inquire about
their volume discount prices that would make a combined package of
products more valuable and profitable.

"It has to be a real and legitimate desire to purchase their products, not
just a ploy," he says. "The revelation to me was that it was much easier to
get higher up in the executive chain in a company as a customer than I
could as someone trying to sell them something." Eliot approached the
maker of a protective liquid sold to auto detailers and repair shops to inquire about the price for a large quantity purchase. Only when the company
representative asked did he reveal the product he was manufacturing. "It
sparks interest when you have something a little secret," he says. "I pur-

posely was evasive and that seemed to intrigue them." The sales representatives referred him to the company president. "When I call as the customer like that I have to sound credible, not like a ding-a-ling inventor who doesn't really have a doable product," Eliot says. "I'm the president of a company and I need this much of this component at this price by this date. I'm 100 percent honest with them." Eliot's timing was fortunate with the auto protective product manufacturer, which was trying to expand into the mass market. The president thought the applicator could be a helpful vehicle in that effort. Rather than sell his liquid to Eliot, the president agreed to license the applicator with a $50,000 up-front payment plus royalties.

"If you're reasonable, you can go a long way toward forming an alliance or structuring a deal or even selling or licensing your product if you are going in from the perspective of a buyer, not a seller," Eliot says.

■ ■ ■

Key elements of a licensing agreement:

■ Identities of the licensing entity and licensee

■ Definition of the invention to be licensed and your rights to this invention (such as a patent)

■ The products in which your invention will be used

■ Any copyrights or trademarks accompanying the license

■ Specific rights being granted (such as exclusive or nonexclusive, geographic limitations, or industry limitations)

■ Any rights reserved to the licensor

■ Length of the agreement

■ Conditions under which the license can be terminated

■ Any right of renewal of the license after the term expires

■ Advances and royalties

100. GET A FOOT IN THE DOOR AND UPSELL

Give customers an introduction to your products
and services and then allow them to make
additional commitments as trust builds.

■ ■ ■

Many business owners think they don't have the time or need for a business coach. But that doesn't stop Laguna Hills, California, coach and writer Roslyn Cerro Schryver. She offers to prepare a one-page business bio that is a great marketing tool for these owners. "It's a fabulous seller when they go to networking meetings," Roz says. "They can carry a stack in their car [and] put the bio out on a table at meetings. When a person throws a business card in their face, they can say, 'If you would like to know more about me, I have this one sheet,' and it's so much better than a card." The one-page bio is a seller for Roz too. She is providing an easily affordable initial product with which she can move the client to the next step of writing a business plan and then to ongoing business coaching. The process of developing the information for the one-page bio helps the client hone in on what they really do and is the first step to writing a business plan.

Many types of businesses find ways to encourage customers to buy more once they dip a toe in the water. In the restaurant business it's called *upselling,* which anyone who ever worked the counter at McDonald's knows. Do you want fries with that hamburger? Roz estimates that perhaps 40 percent of those who hire her to write a one-page bio for them eventually ask her to do more intensive planning work for their companies or careers. "Many of my clients do have a business plan, but they're not working it like they should," she says. "Or I have others who say they want to get out of their business. We develop the plan to get the business in shape to sell, and they get to work. They call six or seven weeks later and say, 'Business has grown 17 percent; I don't want to sell anymore.'"

If a client commits to business coaching, Roz insists on a minimum of three months. Most do not want to make that length of commitment until they build a relationship with her. "There's a lack of comfort. I ask powerful questions that make people think," she says. "Of course, as my business and reputation have grown, I've been able to become more of a risk taker. I offer services now that I didn't when I started."

■ ■ ■

Ways to offer graduated commitment to your products or services:

■ For services, establish a minimal introductory level whose payment can be credited toward long-term or expert level programs.

■ Offer one price for first-time service and a lower per-session price for a 12-month contract.

■ Give a free introductory assessment with a list of recommended actions clients can attempt themselves or with your help.

■ Offer lower prices for members of a frequent buyer or good customer club.

■ When taking an order always suggest a complementary product or ancillary service as well.

101. TEST, TEST, TEST

Test every aspect of your marketing before making
major commitments that could be costly errors.

■ ■ ■

Arthur Gabriele started selling informational products by mail order in 1991 through his company, Catalogs, in Woodhaven, New York. But he didn't take anything for granted. Before he invested heavily in anything from advertising to inventory, he experimented. "All new businesses must start with tests," he says. "My first direct mailing was a test just to see the results. The results were favorable. This told me I was on course, so I built onto my business."

He started with 14 different how-to products about different business start-up opportunities. He tested advertising in various business magazines of various specialties and sizes of circulation. He also tried different sizes of ads and different messages. "Text ads didn't work too well," Arthur recalls. "Maybe people don't respect them as much as display ads." A successful advertisement isn't merely the cheapest one, he stresses. It is the one that brings the highest return on investment. Sometimes a costlier ad in the magazine with the right focus is the biggest winner. On the other hand, Arthur has found that ads in magazines with millions of subscribers but an untargeted focus are a poor investment for him.

Once Arthur crafts just the right copy for an ad in just the right magazine, the results pour in and he repeats that successful ad until it doesn't work anymore. Nothing works all the time or forever. Arthur has successfully duplicated his testing strategy for different mail order products, including health products, and even catalogs of various types of products and business opportunities. In 1997, Arthur tested a Web site. "I started with a free site where I could get the feel for the Internet. Once I knew my site had potential and was bringing in sales that told me it was time to upgrade."

But Arthur continues with his off-line mail order business, sending catalogs to people who have purchased from him in the past. Here again, he tries different messages and different offers, and he continues to test. But when testing, you should change only one element per test. Don't change the message and the name. You won't know which is responsible for the difference. Pricing is the most frequently tested part of a mail-order sales message. Perhaps a third of the mail list receives an offer of two items for the price of one. Another third is offered a 20 percent discount, and the final third is offered the product at its regular price. Surprisingly, sellers of informational products in particular often find that more people will buy at a high price than a low one, perhaps believing that they get what they pay for. Even after years of experience, Arthur continues his habit of testing. "I am always testing something," he says. "I have to check to see what people actually want. My motto is Improve. Improve."

■ ■ ■

Ways to test your marketing:

■ Mail to a portion of a mailing list before buying 100,000 names.

■ To test price point, send ads to three different test groups with the price being the only difference in each ad. Don't try to test more than one fact in a single mailing.

■ Test color versus black and white.

■ Use different cover letters that stress different aspects of your product or service.

■ Compare the response rate from a short sales letter or e-mail to a long one.

■ Try a minimal-cost Web site before investing in an expensive site with Java Script and Flash.

■ Evaluate responses to different Web site designs.

■ Attempt different voice mail messages and on-hold telephone messages.

■ When weighing test results, don't just compare immediate results, but also look at reorder rates or add-on purchases with the basic order.

■ Remove a product from your inventory and see if customers notice.

■ Group different merchandise together in store displays or Web site photos to see if that affects crossover sales.

■ Use different follow-up techniques to find the one that closes the most sales.

THE MARKETING PLAN

A basic marketing plan contains details that focus the effort and how it will be carried out. It cannot be written properly without research. The plan should include information on each of these subjects:

- *Executive summary.* What marketing you will do and why?
- *Your company.* Where are you located? What is your pricing strategy? What's your position in the market? How will you distribute your product or service?
- *Product or service.* What are you selling? What's unique about this product or service that gives it a competitive edge in the market? What are its benefits to the customer?
- *Customer.* What market niche or segment are you targeting? Who is most likely to buy your product or service? Who knows he or she has a need or desire for it and is willing and ready to pay for it? Where are they located?
- *Competition.* Who else is after the same consumer dollar? It might be direct competitors (you sell soda and so do they) or indirect (you sell soda and they sell water or iced tea). Why do customers buy from them? What is their market share?
- *Other obstacles.* Other than competitors, what else will prevent customers from buying from you? Can't get into stores? No name recognition?
- *Opportunities.* What opportunities help you overcome obstacles? "I don't have enough money, but I do have strong relationships with XYZ buyers or a dedicated and tireless sales force." "The well-established, big competitors refuse to take orders under $10,000."
- *Goal.* What do you want to achieve in three to five years? Be specific.

- Strategy. What is your plan of action or system for achieving your long-range objectives? If the goal is to increase profits, the strategy might be to attract more wealthy clients.
- *Tactics or tools.* What are your specific means to achieve your strategy and goals? What are the promotional activities and marketing materials that will carry out the strategy? If you want to attract more wealthy clients, you might offer top quality, extra service, etc.
- *People.* Who is responsible for each action?
- *Calendar.* When will you do each event or activity? Be specific. Review at least monthly to make sure you are on track or if a scheduled activity needs to be modified.
- *Budget.* How much money, time, staffing, etc., will you devote to each marketing activity?
- *Spending.* How are your dollars being spent? Evaluate monthly, quarterly, and yearly.
- *Supporting documents.* Which additional document will help support your plan? Market research reports, customer surveys, competitor evaluation sheets, market trends, etc.?

THE PRESS RELEASE

Fill in the fields like this to create your own press release.

Company Name
Address, Phone, Web Site

Contact:
Name
Phone
Cell phone
E-mail address
(Make sure this person is available)

Release date: (*or* For Immediate Release)

XYZ LAB CLONES SHAKESPEARE

(This is your grabber headline; don't waste it.)

**Great author's DNA preserved from burial will
be used to develop a new race of writers.**

*(This is your grabber subhead providing more information that will get the editor or reporter
to continue reading your press release rather than throwing it in the trash.)*

Put the absolutely most important thing about this story in this first sentence. Do not lead the sentence with the name of the company owner, no matter how much he pays or threatens you, not even if you are the owner. Include in this paragraph any time factor or date important to the story.

The second most compelling fact about this story should start off the second paragraph, and so on through the release. You must tell the reader who, what, when, where, why, and how.

You must emphasize what the benefit is to the reader, listener, or viewer.

Keep the press release to one or two pages.

Check grammar and spelling, especially of names and places. Computer programs that check spelling usually aren't accurate for proper names, so be sure to double-check them for accuracy.

When sending out your press release, find out how your target editor or reporter prefers to receive press releases: e-mail, fax, or postal mail.

Mention any graphic or visual material you can offer if needed. If the story you're pitching is about someone other than the contact person, include his or her contact information in the final paragraph. Make sure the contact's assistants know this release has been sent so they will make a special effort to connect the reporter and news source quickly.

UNDERSTAND WHAT NEWS MEDIA WANT

Third-party media coverage of you, your business, or your products and services can build your credibility, gain recognition, build your prestige, and establish you as an expert. However, everyone else is trying to get publicity too. Attention to detail can help you stand out from the others and enjoy greater success in the publicity game.

Understand What News Is

When creating a news story, editors and reporters will be looking for the following elements:

- *Proximity.* The closer (geographically, in area of interest, or philosophically) the topic is, the more interested the audience will be.
- *Rarity*
- *Effect.* The greater or more widespread the impact, the more the audience wants to know.
- *Prominence.* Well-known people and places attract attention.
- *Significance.* How important is the event to the media source or audience?
- *Information*

- *Entertainment*

Note: Even if your story matches several of these categories, it could lose out to an even bigger story on any given day.

Set Aside Unreasonable Expectations

Keep these points in mind when submitting a press release or story idea to the media.

- Be thankful if the story runs at all. Being the lead story is icing.
- Never expect coverage of a ribbon cutting.
- You're not likely to be the only source or subject in a published story.
- Not everything you want to be in the story will make it; some of what you don't want, will.
- The quotes may be accurate but not quite what you meant.
- The photo won't capture your resemblance to Mel Gibson or Sandra Bullock.

Target the Medium and Outlet

Follow these guidelines to ensure the medium and its target audience are a match for your product or service.

- Pitch your story only to the media watched or read by the audience you want to reach.
- International and national television or radio shows and publications have more stories vying for their attention.
- It might be a curse to receive widespread coverage if you're not set up to accept orders from India or Maine.
- Don't ignore trade publications, specialty Web sites, and cable TV shows which may be the best outlets to reach your target.

Further Narrow Your Media Target

Follow these guidelines when choosing the appropriate editor or reporter to which you will submit your press release.

- Not every section within a publication or every program on a broadcast station is appropriate for your story.
- Look for the right feature within a section: a calendar for an event, a people column for promotions and awards, etc.
- Find the right editor of the section and feature you want to target or the reporter who handles the subject of your story.

Write It Yourself

To increase the chances that your information will be reported accurately, you might consider submitting the finished story directly to the media, however:

- Look for publications that accept freelance stories. Web sites are especially receptive.
- Avoid self-promotion.
- Look for opportunities to be an expert on radio and television talk shows.

Clarify Your Story

Follow these tips to increase the chances of your story being reported.

- Describe your story in a sentence or two in such compelling terms that everyone who hears it will say, "WOW," but don't hype.
- Define your story in terms of what's in it for the reader.
- You have five seconds to grab an editor or reporter's attention.

Offer Value-Added Information

Additional supporting material may increase interest in publishing or broadcasting your story.

- Find information suitable for charts, graphs, tip sheets, and other visual elements.

■ Be prepared to suggest interesting photo opportunities.

■ Prepare a list of other experts on the subject with contact information.

Be Available

Editors or reporters may want to call to verify the information in your press release, so remember:

■ Always include complete contact information: name of the person who is most readily available and knowledgeable, phone number, cell phone number, and e-mail address.

■ Return phone calls and e-mails as soon as possible but no later than 24 hours.

■ If you can't be available, find a colleague who can. If you blow this opportunity, you aren't likely to get another. But if you satisfy reporters or editors' need, they're likely to call again and share your name with other news people.

WEB SITES OF BUSINESSES IN THIS BOOK

1. Commerce Technologies (http://www.commercetech.net)
2. Martin Integrated Systems (http://www.martinintegrated.com)
3. New Millennium Consulting (http://www.nmcstrategy.com)
4. Intuit Inc. (http://www.intuit.com)
7. Dinotown (http://www.dinotown.com)
8. Strata-Media Inc. (http://www.strata-media.com)
9. Paul Reed Smith Guitars (http://www.prsguitars.com)
10. Principal Technical Services (http://www.ptsstaffing.com)
11. Concorde Dental (http://concorde.exceptionalpractice.com)
12. Trilogy Coaching Institute (http://www.highimpactcoaching.com)
13. Southwest Financial Services (http://www.sffinancialgroup.com)
14. NoUVIR Research (http://www.nouvir.com)
15. Snapware (http://www.snapware.com)
16. WOW! Unlimited (http://www.wowunlimited.com)
17. NameStormers (http://www.namestormers.com)
18. Bob Siemon Designs (http://www.bobsiemon.com)
19. Animalmania (http://www.animals.com)
20. Sarris Candies (http://www.sarriscandies.com)
22. OneTone Telecom Inc. (http://www.1tone.net)
24. Schoch Harley-Davidson/Buell (http://www.harleyclothes.com)
26. Boise Paper (http://www.boisepaper.com)
27. DataFlow/Alaska Inc. (http://www.dataflowalaska.com)
29. Pro-Team Inc. (http://www.proteamvacs.com)
30. eHobbies (http://www.ehobbies.com)

31. O & H Danish Bakery (http://www.ohdanishbakery.com)

32. The Telephone Doctor (http://www.telephonedoctor.com)

33. Martin Investigative Service (http://www.martinpi.com)

34. Stockdale Associates Inc. (http://www.stockdale-inc.com)

35. North Wind Inc. (http://www.nwindenv.com)

36. Money Concepts FPC (http://www.moneyconcepts.com)

37. Plums Café & Catering (http://www.plumscafe.com)

38. Rich Mar Shirts and Signs (http://www.richmarsigns.com)

40. Source Diversified Inc. (http://www.sourced.com)

42. Buckley's Mixture (http://www.buckleys.com)

43. Bioanalytical Systems Inc. (http://www.bioanalytical.com)

44. The Catered Affair (http://www.thecateredaffair.com)

45. Cristek Interconnects Inc. (http://www.cristek.com)

46. Back Be Nimble (http://www.backbenimble.com)

47. Liquidity Services Inc. (http://www.liquidation.com)

48. Till Kahrs (http://www.publicspeakingskills.com)

49. Wilson Internet Services (http://www.wilsonweb.com)

50. DealTree Inc. (http://www.dealtree.com)

51. Exceptional Sales Performance (http://www.exceptionalsales.com)

52. MyWrapper.com (http://www.mywrapper.com)

53. Broadband Wireless Exchange Inc. (http://www.bbwexchange.com)

54. Bob Leduc (http://www.bobleduc.com)

55. Ernie the Attorney blog (http://radio.weblogs.com/0104634)

56. StreetGlow Inc. (http://www.streetglow.com)

57. Valuation Professionals Inc. (http://www.valuationpro.com)

59. Carmin Industries (http://www.waterjet.net)

60. The Wine Club (http://www.thewineclub.com)

61. Femail Creations (http://www.femailcreations.com)

62. Maine Balsam Fir Products Inc. (http://www.mainebalsam.com)

63. InLynx (http://www.inlynx.com)

64. Pragmatic Systems & Staffing LLC (http://www.pragmaticsys.com)

65. Home Remedies of NY Inc. (http://www.homereferralbiz.com)

66. Realityworks Inc. (http://www.realityworksinc.com)

67. Challenger, Gray & Christmas Inc. (http://www.challengergray.com)

70. Echelon Biosciences (http://www.echelon-inc.com)

71. Lucius Studio (http://www.luciusstudio.com)

72. The Computer Tutor (http://www.computertutortraining.com)

73. Intelligraphics (http://www.killermarketing.com)

74. Amden Corporation (http://www.amdencorp.com)

75. Manhattan West Mortgage (http://www.manhattanwestmortgage.com)

77. Patent Law & Venture Group (http://www.patentdesk.com)

79. RWR Marketing (http://www.rwrmarketing.com)

80. Marla's Mania (http://www.marlasmania.com)

81. Bob's Aircraft Documentation (http://www.bobsairdoc.com)

83. My Very Own Inc. (http://www.lovecharlie.com)

84. Wall Drug (http://www.walldrug.com)

85. Chutter General Store (http://www.chutter.com)

86. Planet Rascal Inc. (http://www.planetrascals.com)

88. Syagen Technology Inc. (http://www.syagen.com)

89. Aralyn Hughes Realtor (http://www.aralyn.com)

90. Execuplan (http://www.execuplan.com)

91. Motoring Services Auto Repair (http://www.motoringservices.net)

92. Sunshine Makers Inc. (http://www.simplegreen.com)

93. Wet Seal Inc. (http://www.wetseal.com)

95. Solutions At Work LLC (http://www.solutionswork.com)

96. Tapes II International (http://www.tapes2.com)

97. Kink Inc. (http://www.kinkbmx.com)

98. Marketive Inc. (http://www.marketive.com)

99. Eliot James Enterprises (http://www.ejeinc.com)

101. Catalogs (http://www.catalogofcatalogs.com)

Share the message!

Bulk discounts
Discounts start at only 10 copies. Save up to 55% off retail price.

Custom publishing
Private label a cover with your organization's name and logo. Or, tailor information to your needs with a custom pamphlet that highlights specific chapters.

Ancillaries
Workshop outlines, videos, and other products are available on select titles.

Dynamic speakers
Engaging authors are available to share their expertise and insight at your event.

Call Dearborn Trade Special Sales at 1-800-245-BOOK (2665) or e-mail trade@dearborn.com

Dearborn™
Trade Publishing
A **Kaplan Professional** Company